STOP, ASK, and LISTEN

Proven Sales Techniques to Turn Browsers Into Buyers

SECOND EDITION

Kelley Robertson

WILEY

John Wiley & Sons Canada, Ltd.

Praise for Kelley Robertson and Stop, Ask and Listen

People will pay a premium for quality. We've used concepts similar to what Kelley presents in *Stop, Ask, and Listen* and they have helped us succeed. If they work for us, they'll work for you. I recommend this book to anyone who is serious about increasing sales and customer loyalty.

> — *Harry Rosen, Chairman, Harry Rosen Inc.*

This book gives every sales professional, in any market, a step-by-step process to make more sales, faster and easier than ever before. Worth its weight in gold!

> — *Brian Tracy, President, Brian Tracy International*
> *Author of* Advanced Selling Strategies

Stop, Ask, and Listen is an outstanding book! I was amazed how many practical ideas were included. When you apply these concepts you will definitely separate yourself from your competitors. I highly recommend this book to anyone in sales.

> — *Jim Clemmer, President, The Clemmer Group*
> *Author of* Pathways to Performance *and*
> Growing the Distance

I have been exposed to many sales processes and I have never seen one as practical and achievable as Kelley's. It is refreshing to read a book on sales that succeeds in selling me on the process it prescribes. *Stop, Ask, and Listen* combines the essential mechanics and the crucial mindset of successful selling in a process that is totally achievable.

> — *Blair Minnes, Account Manager, Larter Creative*

Stop, Ask, and Listen is an excellent book! Kelley has done what most authors neglect to do—include a step-by-step blueprint to implement the concepts in his book. His examples, analogies, and real-life situations reflect a keen understanding of professional selling behaviour. Good material for salespeople at all levels, whether selling a Walkman or a multi-million dollar aircraft.

> — *Greg Marlo, Director of Sales & Marketing,*
> *OurPLANE Inc.*

Stop, Ask, and Listen is well-written book and a must-read for any salesperson. When you apply the concepts you will demonstrate to your customer why they should buy from you, at your price. It will definitely increase your negotiating power.
— *Michael Sloopka, President, Selling Solutions*

I am reading, re-reading, and re-reading this book. I am convinced that there is no finer book on effective selling in existence! Because of this book, I see a bright future ahead for me in sales.
— *Dave Smith, Sales Associate, Forshey Piano Company*

I have studied this book from cover to cover numerous times and have to say that it is probably the most helpful self-help sales training book I have read so far. My sales results from the open houses increased exponentially this last weekend…thanks to your blueprint. Looks like my sales are on an upward swing!
— *Dino DiDiodoro, Agent, Re/Max Real Estate*

I have read books by the top motivators such as Brian Tracy and Tom Hopkins and *Stop, Ask, and Listen* rates as one of the best. I have already doubled my sales from last month!
— *David Hannah, Sales Consultant, Ottawa West Hyundai*

"*Brilliant*" is the only way to describe this book. Kelley has identified the most significant challenges faced by salespeople and demonstrated how to overcome them. He demonstrates a keen insight into customer needs and wants. All salespeople could learn something from this book regardless of what, and to whom, they sell.
— *Andrea Nierenberg, The Nierenberg Group*

In today's economy, customers are more discriminating and have more information and choice. Kelley's vision and concepts for motivating your customers to buy are unique and practical. This foolproof method of selling will distinguish you from your competition. *Stop, Ask, and Listen* is guaranteed to propel you to the highest level of success.
— *Roz Usheroff, President, The Usheroff Institute*

National Library of Canada Cataloguing in Publication

Robertson, Kelley

Stop, ask and listen : proven sales techniques for turning browsers into buyers / Kelley Robertson. -- 2nd ed.

Includes index.

ISBN 0-470-83367-X

Selling. I. Title

HF5438.25.R6195 2004   658.8   C2003-907496-X

Production Credits
Cover and interior design: Interrobang Graphic Design Inc.
Printer: Tri-Graphic Printing

Printed in Canada
10 9 8 7 6 5 4 3 2 1

Contents

Acknowledgements

The publication of this book represents some very unique circumstances. Just a few short months after the first edition was released, my publisher declared bankruptcy. This meant I was faced with the choice of self-publishing or seeking out another publisher.

I seriously considered taking the self-publishing route until my wife, Louise, encouraged me to approach publishers and explain my circumstances. It was through this support and encouragement I eventually connected with John Wiley and Sons. Without her suggestion and encouragement, this edition would not likely have been produced. Thank-you Louise!

Although writing a second edition of a book does not require the same effort from the author as the original version, it still demands the support and assistance of many other individuals. Several people at John Wiley were instrumental in the production of this book. Karen Milner, championed my proposal and helped an idea become reality. She responded to every e-mail and voice mail message I left and kept me informed with the status of the manuscript. Elizabeth McCurdy was tireless in her efforts to create a great looking book and she caught several inconsistencies in the layout before it went to print. The eagle eyes of copy editor, Martha Wilson, noticed mistakes that everyone missed and made the book more reader-friendly.

I must thank all the people who have attended my training workshops in the last few years. Your willingness to share your challenges encouraged me to research new topics and helped me create new content for this edition.

Finally, I extend a heartfelt thank-you to everyone who purchased a copy of the first edition of this book. Every fax, e-mail and letter telling me about the results you achieved after reading it inspired me.

Introduction

Many books have been written about sales. They tell you the importance of prospecting and how to overcome objections. They discuss closing techniques—usually at great length. They talk about creating a unique selling proposition and how to demonstrate, to your advantage, the difference between yourself and your competitor to your customers.

All of these books are valuable. Unfortunately, they seldom explain how to deal with a real-life average Joe or Jo, the regular consumer who buys from a retailer. They don't discuss the unique challenges that face employees in retail, such as having several competitors within walking distance.

Retailers employ millions of people in North America. Few of them receive much formal training on how to sell effectively. Sure, appliance shops, stereo houses, car dealers, and carpet dealers teach their people how to close, close, close, usually at any cost, just to prevent the prospective customer from leaving the store. Unfortunately, most sales staff are left to figure things out for themselves.

This book was designed with these people in mind. It was written from a sales professional's perspective as well as from a customer's point of view. Whether retail is your chosen career (hopefully it will be), or you are working in that area until something more lucrative comes along, this book will benefit you. It teaches you how to become successful at selling, and also how you can apply these skills to your everyday life. Many people enjoy comfortable lives and earn respectable incomes in retail. Simply buying this book indicates that you want to achieve more. *Stop, Ask, and Listen* will help you accomplish your goal.

Although this book was written primarily with retail salespeople in mind, the concepts in it are useful for anyone who sells for a living. Outside and business-to-business salespeople have found value in the principles discussed in the following pages. If your goal is to improve your sales and increase customer loyalty, this book is for you.

Almost a decade of retail sales training and a lifetime of being a consumer have taught me a few essential points that, when properly applied, will have a tremendous impact on your business. If you apply the concepts on the following pages you *will* see your sales increase. The level at which you apply and execute these concepts, the type of retailer you work for, and your willingness to discard old habits and practise new ones will help determine how much your sales will increase.

This book differs from others you might have read about sales in that you are going to become an active participant in learning, not a passive reader. You are expected to work. Throughout the book you will find a variety of exercises that will make you think, write, and plan. I strongly urge you to work your way through these exercises—they are designed to help you grasp the concepts more effectively.

Reread the title of this book: *Stop, Ask, and Listen*. We often rush into a sale without considering these words. We don't consider our customers' state of mind or what they may be thinking. We seldom pay attention to the signals and clues they give us. We will discuss the significance of stopping, asking, and listening and how these three words can help you increase your sales.

Sales success does not require a degree in nuclear physics. Your age has little or no bearing on your results. Your previous experience does not matter. What does make a difference is your willingness to work. To get the most out of this book, visit www.stopasklisten.com and print the free action planner that is available. This planner is broken down by chapter and includes all of the exercises contained here.

Stop, Ask, and Listen presents a unique approach to the sales process that dramatically alters the dynamics of the customer/salesperson relationship and outlines a five-step process that can be incorporated into most sales structures.

You will learn how your personal attitude affects your sales, how to maintain a positive, healthy outlook at all times, and how to deal with the mental baggage you drag along to each sales interaction. You'll examine what factors influence your attitude and discover ways to change or control them, as well as recognize the difference between a sales professional and salesperson.

I cover ways to create a dynamic and uniquely different first impression and to overcome and prevent the dreaded "Just looking" response. There are tips on separating buyers from lookers in under three minutes, on establishing a rapport with almost any customer, on dealing with customers of the opposite sex, and on identifying the best qualifying questions to ask and how to use them effectively. I guarantee you will learn how to maintain your customer's attention and interest during your entire presentation! You will find ways to paint mental pictures to stimulate your customer's imagination and ways to avoid the most common mistakes salespeople make.

You will learn four simple steps that will enable you to handle any objection effectively, as well as how to determine the real objection—in any sales situation. Later chapters describe dealing with the price objection and offer responses to the most frequently heard objections. You'll learn 14 closing techniques, how to ask for the sale without offending your customer, how to use the power of silence to close more sales, and how to understand your customers and their personal fears. To make the most of your sales opportunities, I explain why you should sell accessories and how you can do it without seeming pushy. I will provide strategies on improving the sale of intangible items such as extended warranties, maintenance programs, and fabric protection. I will teach you how to ask for referrals, the importance of doing so, and the impact referrals can have on your business. You will also learn the importance of following up after the sale.

You will discover how to harness the power of goals to increase your sales and improve your results. You will learn the best way to set goals and how to create action plans that work.

Additional tips will help you increase your sales and build customer loyalty. Finally, you will discover a foolproof method of implementing all the concepts in the book.

Becoming a top performer is not easy. However, the concepts that you are about to discover are relatively simple to implement. I discovered years ago that what is easy to do is also easy *not* to do. If you are ready to change the way you sell, adopt some new disciplines, practise new concepts, and earn more money, then buckle up! Get ready to Stop, Ask, and Listen!

The GUEST Approach to Selling

"Guests are always welcome."

In recent years many different businesses have begun to approach their clients differently. They are now calling them *guests*, which has been the norm in the hotel industry for decades. Many restaurant chains as well as other businesses use this term. A gas station around the corner from my house boasts a sign on its door that reads, "Welcome, guests."

A simple word like "guest" versus "customer" can make a dramatic difference in the way we perceive the people who pay our salaries. A customer is someone who makes a purchase. A guest is someone we welcome with open arms and look forward to interacting with. A guest is more of a friend, someone we will treat with dignity and respect.

I'm not suggesting that you immediately begin calling all of your customers guests. What I would like to introduce to you is the GUEST model of selling. GUEST is an acronym for a five-step sales process.

1. **G**reeting your customers.

2. **U**ncovering the customers' needs.

3. **E**xplaining the product or service.

4. **S**olving objections.

5. **T**elling them to buy.

Many sales-based organizations have their own sales model or structure. The GUEST model is designed to fit into most sales cycles. These five steps are the key components to all successful retail selling. The majority of salespeople in retail don't follow any structured process, preferring to allow the sale to flow naturally. I've heard many justifications and rationalizations for this:

"You can't follow a structured process."
"Customers just take control of the sales process."
"It takes too long to go through a process like this."
"My store is too busy."
"I'm too busy."
"I've done it my way for years and I've been successful."

The list could go on and on. In fact, I could probably write another book just listing the excuses I've heard from salespeople. Here is the point. The GUEST process works. Ultimately, *you* need to take control of the sales process. If you don't, the customer will, which is what happens in approximately 80 percent of all sales transactions that take place on the retail floor. I have seen salespeople shadow customers around the store trying desperately to sell them something.

News flash! Consumers will not buy from a salesperson they don't trust, don't like, or who doesn't show confidence. I have known salespeople with a tremendous amount of experience and knowledge who can't close the number of sales they are entitled to because they try too hard.

Here's a typical sales story. The customer is looking at a product. The salesperson launches into a canned pitch about the product. The customer asks some questions and expresses some objections. The salesperson tries to overcome or defend the objections. The process ends with the customer saying, "Got a card? I'll be back." These words are the kiss of death in retail because few of these customers ever actually return. The reasons are simple.

- The salesperson did not greet the customer properly.
- The salesperson did not ask the customer any questions.
- The salesperson delivered a rehearsed presentation instead of focusing on the customer's needs.
- The salesperson did not gather sufficient information to overcome the customer's objection.
- The salesperson did not give the customer a reason to make the purchase!

The GUEST approach to selling addresses each of these issues. If you make a conscious effort to apply the concepts in this book you will notice an immediate improvement in your sales. The key is to concentrate on the process rather the outcome. If you work through each step instead of trying to close the sale, you will increase your closing ratio. Too many salespeople work hard to close a sale because they need to reach a certain level of sales to earn commission, their boss is hounding them to close a deal, or they haven't reached their sales quota. The result is a desperate attempt to get the customer to part with their hard-earned money. These customers feel threatened, manipulated, coerced and often leave the store without making any purchase at all.

On the other hand if a salesperson concentrates on the sales process the customer will be more relaxed, feel more comfortable, and will be more likely to buy. In my workshops I encourage salespeople to allow the sale to progress naturally. I instruct them to pay attention to their customers instead of focusing on closing the sale. This runs contrary to most sales training where the emphasis is on closing the sale. My philosophy is that the sale will happen when you put all five components together in a relaxed, comfortable manner.

The average salesperson's sales cycle looks something like this:

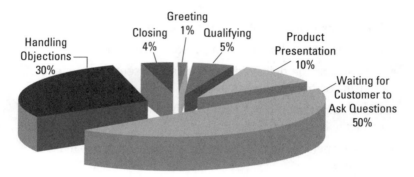

Average Sales Cycle

Half the sale is spent in a passive role! It's no wonder consumers aren't anxious to make a purchase.

Here is the sales cycle of a typical successful salesperson:

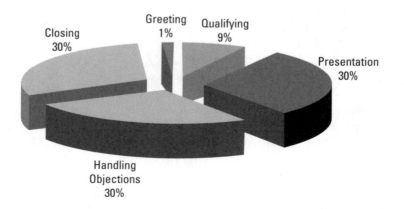

**Typical Sales Cycle
for a Successful Salesperson**

This individual divides his or her time equally among presenting the product, handling objections, and trying to close the sale.

The GUEST model of selling suggests this breakdown:

GUEST Model

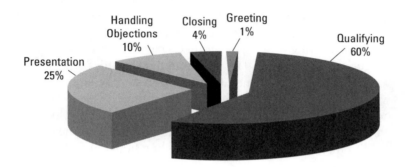

Handling Objections 10%   Closing 4%   Greeting 1%   Qualifying 60%   Presentation 25%

You will notice that most of the time is invested in uncovering the customer's needs. When done properly, this step will eliminate many objections. Unfortunately, most salespeople either don't understand this or refuse to believe it. Most still feel that they have to skate quickly through the qualifying process to have enough time to deal with objections.

A business acquaintance of mine works in advertising. When I approached him to produce a training video he began asking me questions to fully understand what I needed and wanted in a video. Because he took the time to learn about my business needs, I immediately saw the value in this $45,000 investment. Not once did I express an objection about the cost because he demonstrated the value while he uncovered my needs and presented a solution. He made sure that he positioned himself and his company as a problem-solver and a solution-provider.

Another friend of mine owns a training company that provides a variety of training programs to retailers. In his sales training he does not discuss how to overcome objections because he believes, and rightly so, that if you qualify your customer's needs you won't hear any objections. My experience in consulting has confirmed this as well.

As you progress through the book you will begin to see how the GUEST model of selling differs from, and is more effective than, the traditional style. It focuses on the customer rather than on closing the sale. It is designed to make people feel important.

Stop treating your customers like a pay cheque and view them as guests in your store. This may sound awkward, particularly if you have been accustomed to using aggressive selling tactics. If you discipline yourself to follow the blueprint provided here, you will soon notice a difference in the way your customers respond to you. In return, they will be more willing to part with their hard-earned money. They will be willing to buy from you—today—at your price!

Powering Up Your Personal Attitude

"Attitude is a little thing that makes a huge difference."

It has been said that attitude determines altitude. Your personal attitude will definitely determine the level of success you attain more than any other factor. Without the right attitude you will be deterred by the smallest obstacles and will give up long before you reach the level of success you deserve. If you don't have the right attitude you will not be willing to accept new challenges that will help you grow and develop. You will also fear the risks that are associated with these new challenges. Although attitude alone will not guarantee you success in sales, without it you may well find success elusive.

Exercise

Let's explore this in a bit more detail. Assume that every letter in the alphabet has a numeric value according to its location. "A" is 1, "B" is 2, "C" is 3, and so on. Take a moment and assign each letter in the word "attitude" its numeric value. Record your answers in your action planner.

Your responses should be A-1, T-20, T-20, I-9, T-20, U-21, D-4, E-5. Now add these figures together and write this number in the circle on your action planner.

If your math was accurate your total should be one hundred. Coincidence? I doubt it very much. This demonstrates that 100 percent of the results we achieve are a direct reflection of our personal attitude. If you begin your day with the attitude that you are going to have a great day regardless of what happens, then you will likely have a great day and good things will happen. On the other hand, if you believe that your day will be one filled with negative situations, then that is what you will attract.

Let's take this a bit further. You are finishing work one evening and a friend you haven't seen in a while calls and invites you out for a drink. You are scheduled to work the next morning but accept the invitation anyway. You justify it by saying, "I haven't seen him in several months. Besides, a couple of drinks won't be too bad." The two of you meet and before you realize it time has slipped past and it is now very late. You realize that by the time you get home you will only get about five hours of sleep. "No problem" you say to yourself. "I've done that lots of times and always felt fine the next day." You arrive home later, set the alarm, and promptly fall asleep.

The next morning the alarm sounds. What is the first thing you do? If you are like most people, you hit the snooze button and go back to sleep. Nine minutes later the alarm beeps and again you tap the snooze button. On the alarm's third warning, you leap out of bed and frantically begin preparing for work. You race to your car thinking that if everything goes right you'll still make it to the store on time. You fire up the engine and notice that the gas gauge is hovering on empty, and recall that in your haste to get home last night, you said to yourself, "I'll fill up on the way to work tomorrow." If you are anything like me this happens more times than you care to admit.

You drive into the corner gas station and are pleasantly surprised to see an empty lane. You pull up to the pump, fill up your car and pay for your gas. You also pick up a coffee and a muffin for breakfast. As you head onto the highway, you look at your watch and think to yourself, "No problem, I've still got time to make it. Yeah, this day's going to turn out all right after all." No sooner have the words flashed through your head when the traffic comes to a grinding halt. You brake suddenly, spilling hot coffee on yourself. Now, you're caught in a traffic jam, *and* you're wearing coffee-stained clothes. You blast your horn in frustration, drum your fingers impatiently on the steering wheel, shout at other motorists in anger, and look repeatedly at your watch, willing time to stop. You realize with a sinking feeling that you are going to be late.

Ten minutes later the traffic begins to clear and you are on your way. However, your frustration does not dissolve. It seems now that whatever lane you move into, you find your way impeded by cars whose drivers choose to drive for the first time in their lives, right in your path. Slow, slow, slow. You weave in and out of lanes hoping to catch a break in the flow. After what seems an eternity, you arrive at the store, fifteen minutes late for your shift. As you rush through the front door your boss looks at you, taps his or her watch, and asks somewhat caustically, "Do you know what time it is?"

Before you answer let me ask you—are you having a bad day? Or are you having a bad start?

Most people will now have a bad day. They will allow the circumstances of the morning to influence their entire day. When the boss questions their tardiness, they respond with, "You won't believe the morning I've had. First my alarm didn't go off" (embellishment #1). "Then my car wouldn't start" (embellishment #2). "And then some jerk cut me off and made me spill my coffee" (embellishment #3). "I got stuck in traffic for half an hour" (embellishment #4). "I'm having an awful day." This story will be repeated several times throughout the day to every co-worker and, in some cases, even to customers. Each time you tell it, you will add even more to it, so that by the end of the day it will sound something like, "I went to bed early last night but I slept in because the power went off in the entire block. My car was vandalized during the night and my coffee cup broke."

Do the other people you tell really care about your problems? Of course they don't. They have enough of their own to worry about. They don't want or need someone else's misery.

If you continue to think about what happened before you arrived at work, what will happen to your sales during the day?

If you're lucky you might close one sale. Then, at the end of the day, when you go home and your spouse or roommate asks how your day went, you'll launch into another tirade. You'll go on about how difficult your customers were, how no one wanted to buy anything, how they tried to grind you on price, and how difficult it is to make a good living in retail. You'll end up reliving the frustration and anger of the morning's events. You create a self-fulfilling prophecy. It's no wonder no one would buy from you. They could probably tell as soon as they entered the store that you were in a foul mood.

A few years ago I encountered an unpleasant flight attendant on a flight I was taking. She became quite indignant over a mistake the airline had made pertaining to my meal. I, in turn, became upset and frustrated because of her attitude and stewed about it for almost thirty minutes. As time progressed I became engrossed in the in-flight movie and forgot all about it. When I arrived home several hours later, my wife asked me about my flight. The innocent question immediately stirred up my feelings of frustration and anger again. Within seconds I was stressed out over something that had happened hours before!

Your goal every day is to maintain a positive attitude through all of this. Accept the consequences for your actions, assume responsibility, and move on. This will prevent your day from becoming negatively influenced.

I am not trying to trivialize an unhappy situation. Bad stuff happens to people all the time, usually at the most inopportune time. It is how we deal with this stuff that makes the difference. If you *respond*, which is positive, you will look for the lesson or learning point in the situation. If you *react*, which is negative, you will add the experience to the mental baggage you carry.

Mental Baggage

Mental baggage is a collection of all the situations we have experienced or encountered during our lifetimes. We carry this baggage around in our heads and draw from it when appropriate situations present themselves. Perhaps you tried to join a school sports team when you were a child. Your athletic abilities in that particular sport were average; you were unable to make the team. You filed away this experience in your subconscious until a similar situation came along. You immediately recalled the previous performance and outcome, and told yourself that you were not capable of successfully meeting the current challenge. Consequently, you did not make the effort required to meet it.

We all carry around this mental baggage. It influences us in everything we do, both in our business and personal lives. How it affects us on the sales floor is very simple.

At one time during our career we have all had to deal with a difficult customer. Let's say he was looking to buy a pair of dress shoes. He was attired in a navy-blue business suit, white shirt, and a maroon tie. His glasses had thick black frames and he displayed an aura of seriousness. After your fitting him with several pairs of shoes, making several trips to the store room, and spending almost an hour with him, he left the store without making a purchase. You shook your head in frustration, repacked all the shoes and returned them to the back room. You also filed away that person's image in your mind. This became mental baggage.

Some time later a completely different person wearing a navy-blue business suit, white shirt, maroon tie, glasses with black frames comes into the store. You immediately—unconsciously—recall the previous customer and remember that he wasted your precious time (your perception). You then make the decision to disregard the new customer. *If* you finally do decide to serve him, your mindset might still be negative because in the back of your mind you "know" that this type of person is just a time-waster. Ultimately, you display this attitude and end up with a potential customer who receives less than satisfactory service from a salesperson with an obvious chip on his shoulder. This customer, in turn, makes the decision *not* to buy from you, confirming your original assumption about him. Mental baggage may consist of customers who have been rude, abrupt, or angry toward you. Baggage can include situations from earlier in our work careers or even from our childhoods.

As time progresses, this mental baggage weighs heavier and heavier. Yet we continue to drag it around with us into every sales situation. Over time our attitude turns sour; we become pessimistic and jaded, and we view most sales transactions as intrusions on our time. Our productivity drops, our perform-ance slides, and our job security is threatened. We become increasingly bitter toward our chosen occupation, the customers we serve, and life in general.

How do we prevent this from happening?

First, carrying around mental baggage is a natural part of being a human being. It is the way we view and deal with our baggage that makes the real difference in our lives. If we look at each experience and consider how we can learn from it, our baggage will have less hold over us. I recall the first paid keynote presentation I gave. I was well prepared, but not in the appropriate manner. The room was an awkward shape and the stage was positioned quite high, something I had never dealt with previously. I was uncomfortable during my presentation and I knew my delivery was affected. Instead of focusing on this after my session, I chose to concentrate on what I learned from the experience.

Second, we must understand that every sales situation is completely different from the others we have experienced.

Third, we must recognize that some of our baggage is out-dated. We may be relying on information that is several years old. This happened to me at the beginning of my career.

When I was twenty-three I was working for a restaurant chain as an assistant manager. I was promoted to general manag-er and lasted less than a year before I was demoted back to an assistant manager. I had proved unable to perform to the compa-ny's expectations. I ended up leaving the company shortly afterwards. For five years I hesitated any time an opportunity for a promotion presented itself; I was not sure I could do it. Finally it dawned on me exactly what I had learned from that experi-ence. I was not the only person responsible for that particular failure, and my leadership and managerial skills had developed since then. Nevertheless, it took me five years to realize it!

Exercise

Take a moment and, in your action planner, list some of the experiences or situations that may be holding you back. In other words, what mental baggage are you carrying around?

Identifying this is the first step to overcoming it. Here are some suggestions for doing so:

1. Realize that the baggage is only mental. You can replace any mental thought with another thought. Replace the negative image or thought with one that demonstrates your ability to succeed at that particular task or issue. Concentrate on creating a positive self-image. When you find yourself resisting new situations or experiences think about what mental baggage may be contributing to this resistance.

2. Evaluate what has changed since your first experience. Remind yourself of your growth and development since then.

3. Determine whether inaction now will exacerbate the consequence you faced earlier. In other words, does the price of avoiding the current situation outweigh the reward you could gain if you chose to tackle the situation?

4. Take action. You always have two choices:

   • Do nothing, which means that you are allowing your mental baggage to dictate your life.

   • Tackle the situation head on. As author and speaker Susan Jeffers says, "Feel the fear and do it anyway." It may be challenging, frightening, and intimidating. However, you will become stronger from tackling the situation.

Choosing to discard your mental baggage is the first major step that will propel you forward. Once you decide not to allow what has happened to you in the past to influence your future, you begin to take control of your life and your circumstances.

Confidence Plus

Taking control of the circumstances and situations around you will develop your self-confidence. When you consider the amount of rejection that many salespeople encounter, the fact that many salespeople lack self-confidence is not surprising. Top-performing people in any industry typically possess a high level of self-confidence. They may not necessarily have possessed this confidence all their lives.

I have not always had a lot of self-confidence. Outwardly I was Mr. Confident while on the inside I seriously doubted my abilities. I had to wrestle with my own mental baggage for years before I became internally confident. Learning to deal with this begins with letting go of our personal baggage. Here are some methods that can help you develop a higher degree of self-confidence.

Affirmations

One of the most powerful tools is affirmations. Simply put, affirmations are statements that we repeat to ourselves frequently. Although many people are familiar with this concept, few actually use it on a regular basis. You may remember the *Saturday Night Live* skit that satirized affirmations. The truth is that affirmations really do work. They are designed to replace feelings of inferiority, doubt, and the lack of self-worth. The way they work is simple; there are only three rules that you need to remember:

1. **Affirmations must be personal.** Only you can develop an affirmation for yourself. When you express it begin with I. For example, "I earn $35,000 a year."

2. **Put affirmations into the present tense.** Avoid saying, "I want to quit smoking." Instead, state, "I enjoy the lifestyle of a non-smoker."

3. **Affirmations must be positive.** Avoid using negative words. For instance, "I don't want to gain more weight" could be phrased as "I look great in a bathing suit."

The next important point of affirmations is that you must repeat them aloud and several times a day. Your goal is to drive this new message deep into your subconscious and replace the other thoughts that occupy your brain with it. The most effective way to do this is through repetition. The more often you repeat an affirmation the more your subconscious goes to work to produce it and make it become a reality.

Sound too simple? I too was skeptical when I first heard about affirmations. Then I decided to try them. I was on my way to an interview for a job I was hungry for. I had to drive for 45 minutes to get there, and during most of it I kept repeating what I wanted the outcome of the interview to be. I envisioned myself in the role I was being interviewed for. I kept that picture focused in my mind and stated my affirmation aloud repeatedly. I told myself this for the next several interviews and a few months later I was hired. Coincidence? Perhaps, but I don't really believe in coincidences. We create our own situations and outcomes. We determine what happens to us.

Here is another example. Eighteen months after beginning this new job I decided to quit smoking. I created several affirmations that reflected the outcome I imagined: "I am a non-smoker." "I enjoy a smoke-free life." "I live the lifestyle of a non-smoker." "I enjoy living as a non-smoker." I repeated these affirmations several times a day, long before the deadline I had set. A few months later I did quit, almost five months sooner than I had originally intended. I also continued to repeat these affirmations for the first month afterwards to help me get through the withdrawal period. Affirmations helped me picture myself as a non-smoker. They helped my subconscious mind make it a reality. For someone who smoked for more than 20 years, this was a challenging picture to create.

You can use affirmations easily to develop self-confidence. First, choose an area in which you wish to increase your self-confidence. For example, you might have a hard time talking to people in a social setting. You could create an affirmation that concentrates on this. *"I carry on intelligent conversations with everyone I meet"* or *"I speak confidently to the people I meet."* The goal is to repeat it out loud as often as you can prior to the event. I have used similar statements prior to attending networking functions and my confidence in these situations has improved dramatically.

You may not see instant results, which is one of the major reasons why people don't accomplish what they truly could. You have programmed your mind to act and think in a certain manner for years. A few statements repeated once or twice are not enough to overcome that entrenched programming. This will require constant repetition. Day after day, over and over again. In this world of get-rich-quick, lose-weight-fast, and solve-credit-problems-instantly, people are looking for easy, immediate results. If they don't see results right away, they figure the process does not work. In fact, you must be prepared to devote considerable time to replacing years of an engrained thought or habit.

After I quit smoking, I craved a cigarette as soon as I got into my car after work, as soon as I finished eating a meal, had a cup of coffee, or drank a beer. I had to get through several months before these cravings subsided. When I felt them coming on, I would think of my affirmation, repeat it, and remind myself that I was a non-smoker. Years after quitting I have still the occasional craving, but it usually disappears quickly. It just takes time to change a habit.

Allow your subconscious the appropriate amount of time to generate the new thought, and to bring into your life events and circumstances consistent with your new thoughts. If you are patient and maintain a regular routine of repeating your affirmations, they *will* happen. The trick, of course, is to convince your conscious mind to believe them.

If you are currently earning $25,000 a year and your goal is to earn $100,000, you must break this goal into digestible, bite-sized chunks first. Don't make that $75,000 leap in one affirmation; your conscious mind will not accept it as being possible. Instead, create several affirmations. Start with the goal of increasing your income to $35,000. Once you achieve this, create a new affirmation with your income at $50,000, and then $75,000. Then make the jump to the final figure. You'll find taking the smaller steps much more effective than trying to make a huge jump all at once.

If you don't believe that affirmations work, that's fine. I don't expect you to accept this concept immediately. But do try using it. Create an affirmation for one small change you would like to make in your life. Repeat it to yourself frequently every day. Be patient. Before long, you will notice the change gradually beginning to happen.

Talk to Me

Another way to build your self-confidence is to change the information you feed yourself. All of us have a little voice inside our head that provides us with a running commentary on everything we do. This self-talk often does us more harm than good. When we make a mistake it will chastise, berate, and criticize us.

When I first heard that roughly 80 percent of our self-talk is negative I was skeptical. Then I began listening to my own self-talk. Sure enough, most of the reinforcement I was giving myself was negative. I consciously tried to change my internal voice to mostly positive comments. Instead of criticizing myself when I did something wrong, I told myself what I learned from the mistake. I focused on something other than criticizing myself. Before long, I found my entire personality changed. I became very positive and optimistic.

This is not as easy as it sounds. Consider the number of negative messages we are exposed to every day: it is little wonder that our self-talk is not the most positive. What do you read when you open a newspaper? When you watch television? When you listen to the radio? Most of the information we receive daily focuses on negative events. We hear about wars, murders, robberies, deaths, political unrest, scandals, labour disputes, and massive casualties from weather catastrophes such as floods and hurricanes. Where's the positive information in a paper? Usually tucked away on page 24 with 12 lines devoted to it. Consider this: would you eat garbage for breakfast, lunch, and dinner? Then why would you fill your head with garbage every day?

Transforming your self-talk from negative to positive is a difficult process that requires constant effort and attention. Begin by telling yourself that you are going to be positive, that you are going to give yourself positive self-talk. Whenever you catch the voice inside your head feeding you negative dialogue, immediately stop and replace it with something positive instead. As time goes on and you become more adept at this, your self-talk will become more positive automatically. You will continue to have negative thoughts. The difference is that when you begin to think them, you will recognize that it is happening and will be able stop it and focus on the positive.

Once you are able to accomplish this you will face another obstacle—other people. Individuals who seem to have been placed on this earth just to make life difficult for us. Some time ago, I worked with a very pessimistic person. Her mission seemed to be to bring me down. In fact, one afternoon she told me that I was not really a positive person. When I asked her what she meant, she answered that no one could be optimistic all the time, so I was just programming myself to be positive. The first words on the tip of my tongue were "Just as you pro-gram yourself to be miserable?" Fortunately, I bit back my response and avoided embarking on a major battle. I smiled and said, "What's wrong with that?" She gave me an evil grin and exclaimed, "Ha! I knew it!" then she walked off, leaving me to figure out exactly what she meant by the last comment.

Negative people will challenge people who display positive mental attitudes. They will try to make you one of them—

miserable and pessimistic. If you succumb to their efforts you will wind up having the life slowly squeezed out of you. I learned this the hard way.

In one of the companies I worked for, one of my co-workers was this type of person. I didn't realize it at the time, but any time I spoke with him, I left feeling miserable, depressed, and discontented with life at work. Several years later I finally realized what had been going on. He had been trying to recruit me into his club! Now I socialize only with positive, energetic, enthusiastic people.

So what does all of this have to do with sales? So far, we've discussed how our personal attitudes affect our results on the floor. We need to prevent our personal baggage from interfering with our decision to try new approaches. We can build up our personal confidence, which will lead to higher sales. We can use affirmations to reinforce specific behaviours we want to develop. We can use positive self-talk to reinforce what we have done well in a sale rather than dwell on what we did wrong.

Each of these elements contributes to developing a healthy, positive, powerful attitude, also known as PMA, or Positive Mental Attitude—the kind of attitude that will help us become successful on the sales floor.

Salesperson versus Sales Professional

The essential difference between a salesperson and a sales professional is attitude:

A sales professional has the attitude of "How can I help someone today?" A salesperson says, "I gotta sell something to someone today."

Their mental attitude is completely different. **A sales professional is people-centred**. A salesperson is self-centred.

A sales professional is focused on helping customers solve a problem or issue. The salesperson is concerned only with closing the sale.

A sales professional qualifies her customers thoroughly and effectively. A salesperson jumps to a product demonstration as quickly as possible.

A sales professional demonstrates enthusiasm and excitement about his products. The salesperson gives the same canned presentation over and over again.

A sales professional is genuinely interested in other people. Salespeople care primarily about themselves.

A sales professional works at cultivating relationships with her clients. Salespeople just want to get through that sale and on to the next one.

A sales professional generates a high level of sales and income. A salesperson struggles to reach his sales targets every month.

A sales professional earns his customer's respect and develops a large customer base. The salesperson looks at each person as a one-time sale and treats that person accordingly.

A sales professional leaves her personal problems at home. A salesperson drags his problems along with him every day.

A sales professional gives the customer plenty of time to talk. A salesperson does most of the talking.

A sales professional's attitude differs completely from that of a salesperson. A sales professional concentrates on the customer while a salesperson concentrates on herself. Many salespeople view themselves as professionals when in fact they are not. Consider the number of people they must talk to in order to reach their monthly quotas, the potential income they are losing, and the enjoyment and fulfillment they are missing. Salespeople can make the transition to sales professional with little difficulty but they must shift the way they do business in their own minds.

Managing Change

At first, this change can be challenging. It means forgetting your own needs and paying attention to those of your customer first.

It means changing the way you conduct yourself on the sales floor. It means adjusting your approach to the way you sell.

For most people, change is difficult. Change means uncertainty. We create routines in everything we do. When we wake up in the morning, we often follow the same routine to prepare for the day. We drive the same route to work. When we arrive at work, we follow the same routine every day. We approach our customers in the same manner. Routines make us feel safe, comfortable. When we attempt to incorporate something new, we break our normal routines and often struggle to make the new process fit in.

Changing our personal attitude and the manner in which we sell is uncomfortable at first. We fight to incorporate the new approach into our existing style. Like the child who changes school in the middle of the year, we feel torn away from our old comfort zone and pushed into something completely foreign. Everything seems out of place. Yet, in fact, we have only tried to change one aspect of what we do.

Relax. Be patient. Give yourself time to become familiar with the new routine. We all require time to adapt. The key is to be open to changing the way you do business. If you resist and say, "We've always done it that way" then you will be lost in the dust of those individuals who are willing to experiment. In today's business world, the survivors are those who are open and receptive to alternative methods.

How does this apply to what we do on the sales floor? Consider for a moment how much the consumers of today differ from those in the past. They are more knowledgeable. They have access to information they never dreamed possible 10 years ago. They read more. They do more research. They're more conscious of price. They demand better service. What was once considered an "extra" is now expected at no additional charge. Consumers will not tolerate a salesperson who boasts about how good he is. They demand proof and will not hesitate to change companies if the one they have been doing business with does not fulfill its end of the agreement.

As sales professionals we must adapt to our customers' changing needs and requirements. We have to listen to what they want.

The demands they make today will pale in comparison to what they will request tomorrow or next week.

An interesting shift has occurred in the last 15 to 20 years. In the early 1980s retailers were focused on the customer. Then, with a booming economy, they forgot about the customer because their businesses were not affected by what they did as salespeople; they could still close sales, people lined up to buy from them. Then the big-box retailers entered the marketplace. They offered consumers amazing prices with little or no service and people flocked—and still flock—to them. Customers love talking about the money they save by shopping this way, and they are willing to accept poor or little service for the savings. However, many other consumers feel left out. They want good value for their money and they also want good service. Because everyone is trying to compete with the big discounters, many retailers have lost sight of the fact that many consumers still crave great service—service they are willing to pay for.

This unfulfilled desire is your opportunity! If you apply the concepts discussed here, you will attract these shoppers to you like moths are attracted to flames. It won't happen overnight. It won't happen without effort. Moreover, it won't happen unless you have the right attitude—the attitude that the customer is supreme. If you are ready to break out of your established routines, implement a few new concepts, and experience some discomfort, I guarantee that you will accomplish some astonishing results.

Change is not as difficult as you might imagine; it is primarily a matter of deciding that you will no longer accept what you do, in the manner that you do it. **You** decide to change your attitude. No one else can do it for you.

Summary

1. Your attitude determines 100 percent of the results you achieve.

2. Respond or react. You can have a bad start or a bad day—the choice is yours.

3. Deal with your mental baggage and prevent it from controlling your life.

4. Use affirmations to develop new skills such as personal self-confidence.

5. Affirmations must be personal, present, positive. *"I am the top salesperson in the store."*

6. Feed your mind positive information. Change your negative self-talk to positive.

7. Understand the fundamental difference between a sales professional and a salesperson: attitude. Are you going to be customer-focused or self-centred?

8. Understand that change is part of the business world as much as it is in the rest of our lives. It always has been and always will be. You can accept change and move forward, or you can remain at the back of the pack. The choice is yours.

Action Plan

In your action planner, answer these questions:

1. What did you learn in this chapter?

2. How will you apply this information?

3. What challenges do you anticipate?

4. How will you face these challenges?

Greeting Your Customer

"You have exactly one opportunity to make a great first impression."

The way a sale begins will often determine the outcome. If you start on the wrong foot you can sour the customer's frame of mind and erase his willingness to do business with you. Yet few salespeople—not sales professionals—concentrate on developing a great first impression. This first impression begins before you speak a single word to your customer. As a customer enters the store he does a quick visual scan. He spots the salespeople and records his first mental picture. That means that whatever you happen to be doing at that precise moment will influence his first impression. Let me paint a scene for you.

It is a typical morning. The store has just opened and you and your co-workers are standing around the sales counter trading war stories or discussing last night's television show or sporting event when a customer walks in.

What's your first physical reaction? If you are like most people, you probably realized that everyone stops talking and looks at the customer.

The customer now has several pairs of eyes on him and feels like a deer caught in the headlights of an oncoming car. You realize your error and you and your co-workers feel as if you have

been caught doing something wrong. You scatter. Now the customer feels like the same lone deer being surrounded by a pack of
hungry wolves. You have not uttered a single word to him and yet
you have managed to put him on the defensive.

What made such a dramatic impression on the customer?
Your actions and your body language. When we communicate
with other people, they interpret our message by our words,
tone of voice, and our body language. Our words account for
only 7 percent of the way people interpret what we say. Our
tone of voice accounts for 38 percent and our body language
takes up the balance of 55 percent. That means that most of our
message is interpreted through non-verbal actions.

Consider how many messages we can deliver without
speaking a single word. You can tell someone to stop by putting
up your hand, palm out. You can advise a co-worker she has a
telephone call through hand gestures. You can roll your eyes to
express frustration. You can show impatience by glancing
repeatedly at your watch. You can deliver all of these messages
effectively without uttering a single word.

Let's look at how our tone can affect how people interpret
what we say. Read these statements aloud placing the emphasis
on the highlighted word.

I didn't take your money.

I *didn't* take your money.

I didn't *take* your money.

I didn't take *your* money.

I didn't take your *money*.

The emphasis in the first statement suggests that someone
else took the money. The second shows defensiveness. The third
could mean that I only borrowed your money while the fourth
implies that I took someone else's money. Finally, the last statement insinuates that I took something, other than your money,
that belongs to you. Exactly the same words are used in every
case, yet they deliver a completely different message each time.

When we are communicating with our customers, we have to be aware of what message we are delivering. For example, if we have just finished dealing with an irate customer, our tone of voice might reflect our own frustration. If we are not careful, the next customer we speak to will notice this frustration and think that it is directed at her personally. Combine this with negative body language and we deliver a negative message to the other person. We have to make a special effort to communicate effectively to our customers. If what we say non-verbally is inconsistent with our oral communication, we are sending our customers the wrong message.

Pay close attention to *the way* you deliver your message. Ensure that your words, tone of voice, and body language are the same as the message you want to deliver. If you are happy to see someone, greet that person with a firm handshake, direct eye contact, a smile, and enthusiasm in your voice.

Before you approach your prospective customer, stop, *look* at him, and consider what approach will be most appropriate with him. Remember that your primary goal is to put the customer in a relaxed state of mind *before* you begin the sales process.

Creating a Great First Impression

People make up to 11 assumptions within 45 seconds of meeting someone for the first time. These assumptions include: intelligence, level of success, education, knowledge, and expertise, to name a few. That means we only have one opportunity to make a great first impression. If we fail to make a positive impact immediately we will have to work harder to establish trust and credibility. Customers' impressions are influenced by our clothes, the way we speak, and how we look and behave.

Yet we often forget the importance of the critical first moment. We may be distracted, tired, frustrated, or not in the proper frame of mind for some reason. The result is a lacklustre first impression. We know the customer is important but all too often we forget to demonstrate it. Here is a simple technique that will help establish a great first impression with a customer:

Maintain the attitude that the customer is really important.

We all know and understand this. Yet in the real world it is easy to forget. Think of times you have been elbow-deep in products, trying to merchandise the store. A customer comes into the store, makes a beeline toward you, and then asks, "Do you work here?" We think to ourselves, "Does it look like I work here?" Then, when we actually do respond, our tone of voice will have a slightly sarcastic or edge to it. We have now announced to the customer, without meaning to, that she is not important.

You only have one chance to make a great first impression. Don't blow it!

"Just Looking"

How many times a day do you hear this? Ten times? Twenty? Fifty? This is by far and away the most common response we hear when we first approach and greet customers. These two words frustrate, annoy, and aggravate us. We feel even worse when we actually greet them and they still breeze past us with "Just looking." They take a few steps and pause as they glance around the store. "Do you have . . . ?" We shake our heads and imagine responding, "If you want . . . why did you say 'Just looking'?"

Before we can effectively overcome this response, we need to understand why people say it. There are two reasons.

First, "Just looking" is a conditioned response. When we were very young our parents took us shopping and we heard them say, "Just looking" when a salesperson approached. We noticed that the salesperson immediately left our parents, allowing them to wander unattended through the store. As we grew older and became independent, we used the same phrase and discovered that it worked just as effectively for us. Now, in most buying situations, the customer has learned to say these words to reduce the pressure they feel from the salesperson.

Second, until the customer actually decides to buy something, he is just looking. Until he makes the buying decision, reaches into his wallet, and pulls out his credit card or cash, *he is just looking!*

So how do you deal with this conditioned response? Use a different greeting! I'm constantly underwhelmed by the lack of thought most salespeople put into their greetings. In most cases they say, "Hi, how are you today?" or grunt, "How ya doing?" A greeting that I really dislike is "How are you *guys* today?" particularly when I am with my wife. Even worse is "youse" guys. Greetings such as these will not help you set yourself and your store apart from your competitors. In fact, as I see it, no salesperson should ever use this type of greeting. It is tired, old, and stimulates no useful response from your customer.

"How are you?" or "Can I help you?" is a conditioned greeting, just as "Just looking" is a conditioned response. If you want to change your customers' response to you, change your greeting to them. Instead of saying some variation on, "Hi, how are you today?" try something different. Comment on her clothing or, if you happen to be in a high-traffic mall, ask about the parking. Be enthusiastic. Mention your store name. *"Hi, welcome to Widget World"* or *"Thank you for coming in to Widget World."* Research has shown that most people shopping in a mall do not remember the name of the last store they shopped in. I noticed this many years ago in myself when I was buying a pair of shoes from a store that was in the mall across from where I lived. I went into this mall several times a week, frequently saw the name of the shoe store on the storefront, and yet I had to ask to whom to make the cheque payable. So try to incorporate your store name into your greeting whenever possible.

You also need a variety of greetings during your workday. Avoid the pitfall of using the same greeting repeatedly. In the early 1980s my wife and I went to a new restaurant with one of our friends. After we were seated our server came over and said, "Hi, my name is Bob. I'll be your waiter tonight. Here's a complimentary snack to get you started. Would you care for a strawberry margarita before dinner?" I didn't think much of it until other customers took their seat at a table close by. The same server approached them and said, "Hi, my name is Bob. I'll be your waiter tonight. Here's a complimentary snack to get you started. Would you care for a strawberry margarita before dinner?" Several minutes later, more customers were seated at another table nearby. Again, the same server. Again, the same greeting. I found myself imitating him every time he approached a new table after that until my wife was kicking me under the table!

Obviously he had been instructed to speak those lines to each new table of customers he greeted. The restaurant was striving for consistency, and in doing so stripped him of his individuality. He displayed no enthusiasm in his voice, no excitement, no energy. His greeting was the same at every table. If we fall into the rut of using the same greeting or approach with all of our customers, we will become boring, as mundane as we sound and we will lose the oomph we need to close the sale. We might have the energy and enthusiasm at nine-thirty in the morning but by the end of the day we are tired and just want to go home. Inevitably, we will issue greetings that come out more like grunts.

In my seminars, I encourage the participants to vary their greetings as soon as they return to their stores. What they generally find is that this reduces the customer's propensity to respond with the dreaded "Just looking." When they approach their customer with a greeting other than "Hi, how are you today?" their customer responds differently as well. Sound too simple? Experiment. Visit your local mall. Walk into 10 or 15 stores and listen to the salespeople's greetings. I assure you that in most cases you will hear the bored, unimaginative approach. If you do, by chance, encounter a greeting that is different, pay attention to your own response to it. I can almost guarantee that it, too, will be different.

With the increase in competition, it has never been more important to differentiate yourself from your competition. A small thing like your greeting makes a significant difference in how people will respond to you.

Types of Greetings

There are two types of greetings you can use: product-focused and social greetings.

Product-focused greetings focus the customer's attention on a specific product or piece of merchandise in your store. For example, "Were you aware that we have the largest selection of . . . in the market?" or "Isn't that a great picture?" or "We offer that model in a variety of colours" or "That model has some new features you might be interested in." This kind of greeting is best used when the customer has been standing by an item for several moments and can be useful in starting the sales process rolling.

On the other hand, you use a social greeting as an icebreaker. Generally it has nothing to do with the sale itself. With this greeting you are simply helping the customer open up and feel comfortable. Some examples include. "Hi, welcome to . . . . How was the parking today?" or "I notice you're wearing a (name the team) jersey/hat. Are you a big fan?" or to someone with a fistful of bags, "It looks like you've been out 'investing' the household budget."

Social greetings vary depending on the situation. They are intended to initiate conversation between you and the customer. I suggest you read your local paper and be aware of events occurring in your community. Even if you are not a sports enthusiast, browse through the sports section and know who won the important games the previous day, particularly if you work in a hardware or sports gear store and the majority of your customers are male. If a customer begins to elaborate on the game and you know nothing about it, admit it: "I don't know much about college ball but I do know that Miami State was favoured to win. You sound as if you follow it pretty closely, though." Then let *them* share *their* knowledge. This actively engages the customer and begins the sales process naturally and comfortably. Plus, it starts the customer talking about something *they* are familiar with. This will help *them* become more comfortable with you and improve your opportunity of closing a sale.

One last comment here. If you vary your greeting with every customer, you will begin to demonstrate that you are different from your competition and you'll begin to give people a reason to buy from you—thus creating customer loyalty.

Overcoming "Just Looking"

If you still get the dreaded "Just looking" response even after you have changed your greeting and approach, here is how to deal with it.

1. Employ humour. You have a number of options with this. You can respond with "Just selling" although this line can backfire if your delivery is not perfect. You could say, "Well, you'll be happy to know that looking is 50 percent cheaper today than it was yesterday." This may elicit a smile from your customer once she processes what you have said. If you can encourage her to smile or laugh, then you have made great progress. You have reduced her defensiveness and begun to establish rapport.

2. Use enthusiasm. "Great. You picked an excellent store to browse in." Then tag this statement with a qualifier such as, "What specifically are you looking for?"

3. Don't allow yourself to be distracted by it. Remember your primary responsibility. Your goal is to make your customer feel comfortable and welcome. Don't allow yourself to become frustrated or annoyed by this conditioned response.

4. Tell yourself that this is a conditioned response and that until a customer actually buys something, she is indeed just looking.

Appearance IS Everything

Your personal appearance will help set the proper tone to the sale. Attire will vary depending on what you do and where you work. Some retailers insist on uniforms; others give their employees free rein to wear what they like. Some require suit and tie, while others accept casual garb. Regardless of your organization's dress code, always strive to look your best. Even if you work in a store that sells jeans, you can still add panache and professionalism to your appearance.

- Avoid garish jewelry unless that is the kind of business you are in.

- Limit your use of colognes and fragrances. Many people are easily offended by perfumes and some are even allergic to them. If you wear a fragrance, don't overdo it.

- Keep your nails and hair neatly trimmed and clean.

- Avoid ultra-trendy clothing unless you work in a store that sells it.

- Never chew gum!

- If you smoke, wash your face and hands immediately after you have a cigarette. The smoke lingers on clothing and skin and many people find it offensive.

- Brush your teeth throughout the day. This will help keep your breath fresh, especially if you drink coffee or smoke.

- If you wear a suit and tie, consider the investment of having your shirts dry cleaned rather than machine-washed. They will look brighter, fresher, and crisper. Have your suits and ties dry cleaned regularly too. Suits should only be dry cleaned three to four times a year. Hang them outside for a few hours each month to freshen them.

- Make sure that your clothing fits you well. Properly hemmed pants, jackets with the correct sleeve length, and shirts with the right collar size all contribute to your professional appearance.

- Polish your shoes regularly and buff them daily.

- Avoid clothing that is worn out. We all have a favourite shirt, sweater, dress, or jacket. Nevertheless, there comes a point at which even our favourite article of clothing becomes too worn for appropriate business use. Recognize when your clothing needs to be replaced and do it.

Although these may seem like common sense suggestions, many salespeople often neglect or overlook them.

A general rule of thumb to follow is, the more expensive the products you sell, the more professional you should look. Like it or not, customers make assumptions about you based on your appearance. When my wife and I were deciding to purchase some new living room furniture I was reluctant to buy from the salesperson helping us because his clothing was outdated. His shoes were scuffed and his sport coat had leather patches on the elbows—I had one similar to his but that was in 1979! I could not help but think to myself, "How can this person help us make a $3,000 purchase when he can't afford a proper wardrobe?"

Acknowledgement

What else can you do to ensure a great first impression on potential customers? Acknowledge them quickly. That does not mean you should pounce on them as soon as they enter the store. Just let them know that you see them. You can do this by making eye contact with them or gesturing with a small wave of your hand or head nod. This accomplishes several things.

First and foremost, it lets customers know that you are aware of their presence. We have all been ignored either in a restaurant or a store and we don't appreciate it.

Second, when you acknowledge a customer's presence, he will wait longer for service than if he has not been acknowledged. If your store is extremely busy, you are engaged with an existing customer, or you are short-staffed, this small courtesy can make a big difference.

Third, it improves security in your store. When an employee greets a potential shoplifter and has made solid eye contact with her, there is less of a chance that that person will try to steal anything.

I am surprised how few salespeople acknowledge new customers when they are engaged in a discussion or presentation with another customer. Perhaps they think that they will offend their current customer if they merely establish eye contact with a new person entering the store.

Another important point: develop a great handshake. Whether you are a man or a woman, ensure an excellent first impression by knowing how to shake hands properly. A good handshake should be firm but not overbearing. Years ago I worked with a supplier who felt he had to crush the other person's hand. Remember, this is an introduction, not a competition. On the opposite end of the scale, avoid a limp, dead fish grip. A good handshake lasts for just a few seconds and requires one to three slight pumps of the wrist and arm. If you truly want to make an impact on your customer, gaze into his eyes and notice their colour as he speaks his name. This will give him the feeling that you are really paying attention to him.

Practise developing your handshake with a friend. Ask him to rate it on a scale of one to ten. If he rates it less than perfect, ask him to tell you what you *specifically* need to improve. Repeat until you have developed the perfect handshake.

Greeting your customer sets the tone for your dealings together and for the remainder of the sales process. Make a positive impression and give your customers a reason to buy from you, today, at your price.

Summary

- Pay close attention to your body language and tone of voice and to those of your customer.
- Be aware of the customer's likely state of mind and adapt your greeting to reflect this.
- Vary your greetings so that you are not using the standard approach of "Hi, how are you today?"
- Shortstop the customer's conditioned response, "Just looking," by avoiding your own conditioned greeting.
- Learn to use different types of greetings, both product-focused and social.

- Ensure your appearance is as professional as possible.
- Acknowledge your customers when they come into the store.
- Develop a great handshake and use it to create a positive first impression.

Action Plan

In your action planner, answer these questions:

1. What did you learn in this chapter?
2. How does this apply to what you do?
3. What will you do differently, beginning today?
4. What challenges do you anticipate and how will you deal with them?

chapter four

Uncovering the Customer's Needs

**"People will tell you anything you want to know—
all you have to do is ask."**

The most important aspect of the sale is qualifying—discovering exactly what the customer needs or wants. Yet the vast majority of salespeople fail to uncover their customers' needs effectively. They ask one or two questions—if any—then they leap into a product presentation.

Why do so few salespeople actually take time to fully understand what their customers are looking for? The most common explanation is that salespeople think that discovering this information will take too long. They know they're going to have to spend time in overcoming the customer's objections. So, rather than take that time to determine a customer's needs, they jump into their presentations with the idea that they will use that time to overcome the customers' objections later. What they don't realize is that if they qualify their prospect accurately and thoroughly, they will receive fewer objections later in the sales process.

Effectively qualifying a customer *does* take time. It takes energy. It takes discipline. You require many skills to uncover a customer's needs effectively. If there is one aspect of selling you should learn to do properly, it is learning to understand your customer.

In Chapter One I introduced the GUEST model of selling, suggesting that you allocate as much as 60 percent of your time to uncovering your customers' needs. In this chapter I will discuss the needs of every customer, what questions to ask and how to ask them, and why you should build rapport with your clientele. I will explore the importance of listening and identifying some of the barriers that prevent us from actively listening to our customers. You will also learn how to tell buyers from lookers within three minutes and see how taking this step can actually prevent customers from voicing some objections. We will also look at the differences between men and women in the buying process.

First, we will examine the customer according to the needs that he or she hopes to satisfy.

The Needs of Every Customer

Every customer comes into your store looking to fulfill two specific needs. The first is a logical need pertaining directly to the product. These can include size, colour, warranty, specifications, power output, energy savings, ease of use, features, price, and so on. Regardless of the product the customer is looking to purchase, she has specific logical needs that must be met.

The second, and often most important, needs are emotional ones. These needs relate to the customer's ego and feelings of satisfaction, relief, success, pride, and joy. These are the needs that usually propel or motivate the customer to buy.

Let's consider a person buying a pair of jeans. Her logical needs may revolve around colour, waist size, leg length, and perhaps price. Her emotional needs will likely focus on how the jeans feel and look on her and perhaps the name of the designer. In most cases, she will ultimately decide whether or not she buys jeans from you based on these latter needs. Colour and size are easy needs to fulfill; the emotional aspect of the purchase can be difficult to determine and satisfy.

Many salespeople are experts at uncovering a customer's logical needs. They ask questions like, "What are you looking for in . . . ?" or "Is this something you'd like?" or "Do you want . . . ?" or "Would you be interested in . . . ?"

While they learn what the customer wants in the product, they don't find out why she is making that particular purchase. They don't ask questions that would give them a better insight into the customer's state of mind. They don't learn what is driving the customer to buy. Determining a customer's emotional needs requires you to get answers to questions like these:

- What is the customer looking for?
- Why is she in store looking for jeans?
- What style of jeans will make her feel good?
- What is her preferred colour and why?

Many salespeople feel that questions such as these are intrusive and that the customer will be offended if asked them. The opposite is actually true.

Most people will tell you anything you want to know. All you have to do is ask. If you demonstrate a genuine interest in your customers, they will respond accordingly and give you information that will help you determine what is truly motivating them to buy. Yet most salespeople see this process as a waste of time and they neglect uncovering this powerful psychological factor in the sales transaction. Never underestimate how a customer wants to feel *after* the purchase is made.

How Much Time to Allow for Qualifying?

There are no hard-and-fast rules about how much time you should take to qualify your customer. Obviously, the larger or more complex the sale, the more questions you should ask. It surprises me that the typical person selling high-ticket items like electronics, appliances, cars, furniture, or computers asks very few questions. He could learn so much more about his prospect if he only took the time to enquire.

This is a simple concept in theory and a challenging one in real life. How often have you been stumped or surprised by an objection at the end of the sale, such as "I need to check with my wife," "I'm going to think about it," or "I'd like to shop around." If you're like most salespeople, this probably happens to you daily. Here are some key questions you can ask to prepare for these objections.

- "Who is involved in this decision other than yourself?"
- "Who else is part of the buying process?"
- "Where else have you been?"
- "How long have you been shopping for this item?"
- "When were you considering making this purchase?"
- "What deadlines are you working with?"

The first two questions will determine who the decision-maker is. Let's assume the customer responds by saying, "My wife." You could continue the qualifying process with, "I notice she's not with you. When were the two of you planning to shop together?" When the prospective customer has responded, you could ask, "What have the two of you discussed about this so far?"

Again, your goal is to learn as much about your prospect as possible. When only one half of a couple is shopping for a major purchase, it is not likely that you will close the sale unless you apply high-pressure sales tactics—which is contrary to the GUEST model of selling. I am not saying that you should not try to close; I am suggesting that closing the sale at this point will be more difficult than it would be if both people were present. However, if you gain this information early in the selling process, you can plan your strategy accordingly and give your prospect a reason to return with his spouse or partner. Here is the strategy you can use to accomplish this:

As I mentioned previously, begin by asking the customer what he and his wife have talked about. Ask him what particular concerns his wife may have, what her interests are, and what is important to her in the purchase. Although he may not have all the answers, it is likely he will have some valuable insight. When you discuss the product later in the sale you can refer to these specific points and tell him what he should say to his wife when he returns home. You should also ask him for his telephone number and request a second meeting. You can do this by asking, "Would it be okay if we arranged a time for your next visit? That will ensure I am here to answer both your questions." Some people will respond favourably, which means you now have a commitment for the couple to return. It is possible they may not show up but, in most cases, they will honour their agreement.

The second pair of questions—"Where else have you been?" and "How long have you been shopping?"—will elicit other important information. If a couple is interested in appliances and yours is the first store they have entered, you will find it virtually impossible to close the sale immediately. This situation does give you a great opportunity, however.

If you do your job exceptionally well, you will give these customers a reason to return since they will be comparing every other store and salesperson they visit to you. Also, before they leave the store you can say, "I'd really appreciate it if you would come back and see me before you make a final decision." This non-threatening approach encourages them to return, giving you the potential opportunity to close the sale later. If the customer responds to the third question by listing several other stores, your next step should be to ask, "What have you seen?" followed by, "What did you like or dislike?" and "What was your experience at . . . ?" Answers to these questions will give you invaluable insight into their buying experiences to this point. You could then say, "You have obviously been shopping around; you must be getting tired of looking. I hope that I can help you make your final decision to buy here at O'Connor's." *Make sure that your tone of voice does not sound aggressive in any way.*

The last set of questions is—"When were you considering making this purchase?" and "What deadlines are you working with?" Sometimes a salesperson spends half an hour to an hour with someone, only to find out later that the customer was not ready to make his purchase for several months. The salesperson gets upset because he feels that the customer has wasted his time. However, the salesperson didn't ask the right questions at the appropriate time. Asking these questions in the manner presented here is very different than asking, "So, if we find the right product are you prepared to buy today?" or "Are you looking to buy today?" or "What will it take to earn your business today?" Typically, retailers who use these tie-down questions are concerned only with closing the sale that day, not with establishing long-term client relationships.

These few questions can help you quickly separate lookers from buyers generally within two or three minutes. A tire kicker will respond to these questions with a quick and flustered, "I'm really just looking. I'm not planning to buy anything." People who do intend to make a purchase will respond with feedback such as:

- "My spouse. I get to do the homework, narrow it down to a couple of choices, then bring her/him with me to make a final decision."
- "We've been to two other stores."
- "I've seen four other models."
- "We're doing some comparison shopping."
- "I need it by next Thursday."

Most salespeople don't ask the right questions to distinguish a qualified buyer from a looker. By asking a few good, open-ended questions you can quickly decide if someone is a qualified prospect.

When my wife and I wanted to purchase a washer and dryer, we visited four different stores. Not one salesperson asked us why we were buying a new set, where we had been, what we had seen, or when we needed the set. In fact, I don't recall hearing a single qualifying question in *any* of the stores. What a lost opportunity to make a difference!

I guarantee that if you ask some thoughtful questions you will begin demonstrating at least one good reason why people should buy from you instead of your competitor.

Managing the Customer

How do you deal with that person who does not plan to make her purchase until sometime in the future? First, ask "When were you planning to make this purchase?" or "What kind of time frame are you considering for this?" Most salespeople don't ask questions like this and they become angry when they find out 20 minutes later that the customer is not planning to buy for six months.

Assuming you have asked the right questions and that the customer has responded along the lines of "We're waiting for our house to be built so we're not going to make a final decision until . . ." here is a simple technique. Say, "I think it's great that you're doing your groundwork now. Could I make a suggestion?" Pause and wait for a positive response. "I'd suggest you wait until you're closer to making that final decision to start doing all your research. Our products change all the time and I'd hate to see you waste your time by having to go through the entire process again in a few months."

This is a subtle way of demonstrating respect—first, by confirming her decision to shop early and, second, by telling her that you would like to save her time. In most cases, people will respond very positively. However, what if the customer does say, "That's okay, we don't mind. Tell me about the . . ." You now have two choices. If your store is very quiet at the time, it may be in your best interest to discuss the product(s) with her in detail.

However, if you are very busy, I recommend you give her whatever written literature is available and say, "I'll be more than happy to answer any questions you might have. Let me take care of those people over there and I'll be right back." This allows you to manage your time effectively and deal with qualified buyers while not alienating the potential customer you already have.

Another challenging person to deal with is the one who comes into your store and asks, "What's the difference between these two items?" or "What's new in . . . ?" Our natural response is to give him the answers to these questions and blab away about our products. There are two ways to respond more effectively:

1. **"There are quite a few differences. Rather than waste your time telling you about all of them, would it be okay if I ask you a few questions? That way I'll be able to show you a product that will suit your needs perfectly."**

2. **"I'd be more than happy to tell you what's new. Before I do that, I'd like to ask you what you're looking for in a . . . "**

Both approaches enable you to maintain control of the sale and gain more information from your customer at the same time. I suspect your initial thought is that the customer won't respond with the information you are requesting. I can tell you from first-hand experience that in most cases they will. People do tend to respond directly to what is asked of them. Customers don't enter the store with the entire script of a sales cycle planned in their head. They come looking for something and expecting a certain approach. If you change your approach, they will change their response accordingly.

Here is yet another challenging person to handle. I am thinking of the customer who breezes into the store, goes directly to a product, and demands of you, "What's your best price for this?" These people are aggressive, abrupt and catch us off guard. Here are some responses you can use.

- **"My best price is (quote full retail). Would you mind if I asked you a few questions to determine if this is the right model for you?"**

- **"My best price is (quote full retail). You seem to have been shopping around. Do you mind if I ask what you've seen?"**

- "My best price is (quote full retail). You seem to know what you're looking for. How did you determine this model is the right one for you?"

Each of these responses is designed to help you gain control of the sales process. If you immediately quote a lower price you still have no idea what prices you are competing against in the customer's mind. You don't know if that particular item is the one most suited to that person's specific needs. You simply don't have enough information!

It is *your* responsibility to maintain control of the sale. If you don't, the customer will take control and in doing so will dictate the outcome. This means that there is less of a chance you will end up accomplishing what *you* want, which is closing the sale. The person asking the questions is in control; the person responding is simply following the questioner's lead. Many salespeople allow the customer to dominate the sales process completely.

I remember working in an electronics store after I had taught one of my workshops. One of the salespeople was hungrily shadowing a husband-and-wife team of would-be customers. He looked like a puppy dog eagerly following his owners and begging for attention. "I need the sale. I need the sale," he seemed to be saying. He apparently lacked confidence, he did not ask any questions, he did not take control of the sale, and he certainly did not establish any form of rapport with those potential customers.

Establishing Rapport

Many people in sales mistakenly think that they have established rapport with a customer once they have made a sale to him. I have noticed many salespeople visibly relax and become more comfortable once the sale is closed. What they don't recognize is that if they build rapport *during* the sales process, then they enable the sale to proceed more naturally and comfortably to this happy conclusion.

Customers, on the other hand, want to feel comfortable *before* they make their purchasing decision. They want the salesperson to listen to them and to pay attention to them. But salespeople are so often preoccupied with closing the sale they miss the customer's signals and clues: signs of impatience, boredom, or frustration.

Usually, the salesperson jumps into a product demonstration and begins rattling off every feature about the product in the belief that she is impressing the buyer with her extensive knowledge. What's actually going through the customer's head is, "God, will this person ever shut up? I just want to get out of here."

Showing your customer that you care about his needs, personal interests, or concerns will help you in developing a good connection with him. Let's say, for example, you are selling appliances such as washers and dryers. When a couple comes into your store, they often feel somewhat irritated. Their dryer has just broken and they need to replace it. They don't anticipate enjoying the experience. In most cases, this expectation is met. Your goal as their salesperson is to change their expectation and *make* their purchase enjoyable. Rather than concentrating strictly on their logical needs—the features they desire—consider discussing other issues with them.

In a gentle, non-threatening manner ask them what happened to their previous unit. Enquire how long they had the machines. Ask them to describe how they typically used them in an average week; for example, how many loads of laundry would they have put through? Where in their house are the machines located? How much space is there around them? Ask them to tell you what they liked most about their old unit. What improvements or features would they like to see in the new one?

These questions should get your customers talking with you. As they explain what they are looking for, they will begin to warm to you, particularly if you are listening to them. Interject an occasional remark to show you are paying attention, nod, smile, and show you empathize with them. The key is to show genuine concern and interest. Listen to what they say and don't be in a rush to begin presenting a particular product before they finish. If, through the natural course of the discussion, you discover that you have something in common with your customers, share it with them. Don't fake it or make up something in the hopes of gaining their trust!

I recall buying new appliances with my wife. At one point in the discussion the salesperson told us he had the same model. Interestingly, I noticed that he averted his gaze and wouldn't make eye contact with us when he said this. I immediately wondered if he was lying. Any credibility he may have built with us to that point was utterly destroyed. From that point on, I distrusted everything he said.

Establishing a bond with someone means you explore areas of common interest. For example, if you work in an electronics store and someone comes in looking for a new television, ask him what type of shows the family watches. If they enjoy some of the same programs you do, you can discuss these, taking the client's mind off the sales transaction for a moment or two. Almost everyone enjoys talking about himself. Encourage your customer to talk about his personal interests. If a prospect tells you that that he is going on vacation, rather than grunting and shifting his attention back to the product, ask where he's going, when he is leaving, what he plans to see and how long he will be away for. Show interest and listen—stay alert. You may hear information that may help you later in the sale.

Establishing rapport will help your customer feel more comfortable with you. I travel by air quite extensively and frequently become engaged in conversation with the person sitting next to me. I have learned more about some people than I ever dreamed possible and, in some cases, more than I wanted to know. One seatmate told me that he recently had a vasectomy, though I had known him for less than half an hour! The point bears repeating: People will tell you absolutely anything you want to know; all you have to do is ask.

This notion remains alien to most salespeople in nearly every business. I frequently hear them protest, "But I really don't care about my customer" or "This will take way too much time" or "People won't tell me that stuff" or "What if I don't have anything in common with them?" These are all valid objections. People feel that way for a reason.

The fact is that most salespeople don't see the value in establishing any kind of relationship with their customers. They think that they will have to become outright friends with them. This is not what I am suggesting. If you show some interest in your customers and the way they live, they will show interest in you and your product.

The result will be a sales transaction that is less stressful to both of you and one that will result in more dollars in your pocket. The additional benefit is that this approach increases customer loyalty.

Keep in mind that establishing this bond with your customers will actually prevent some of their objections before they think of making them. People are less likely to challenge someone they like. Remember that appliance salesperson who I suspected had lied to me? When it came time to negotiate the price and details of the sale, I was ruthless with him. I figured that since he was willing to mislead me in order to get the sale, I would work him over to make sure he really earned my business. Customers react this way instinctively. If you want to reduce the number of price objections the customer will throw at you, concentrate on establishing good relations with her at the outset. Gather as much information about the customer and her purchasing situation as you can.

The drawback in employing this rapport-building approach is that you could find yourself easily sidetracked. Watch that you don't become so involved in a personal discussion that you lose sight of your main objective, which is, after all, closing the sale. I know salespeople who get so caught up in these that they end up losing the sale. Maintain an equal balance between business and social conversation.

Not all customers will open up as readily as you would like and share personal information with you. Some people will interpret your approach as a way to manipulate them into buying something. That's fine. If you are dealing with someone who is not forthcoming with information, someone unwilling to share a personal side, concentrate on drawing out his logical needs instead. If a customer does not want to divulge personal information, focus on the task at hand—demonstrating why he should buy from you—today—at your price.

Quality Qualifying

As noted, accurately assessing your customers' needs requires you to ask them the right questions. Traditionally, salespeople ask the wrong kinds of questions. They ask questions that the customer cannot answer or questions that only require a simple yes or no response. Let's deal first with questions that the customer cannot answer.

The salesperson asks about a particular feature, "Would you like this [technical name]?" Because the customer has not had that particular feature before, he will not know what it will do for him. He really can't answer. He may respond with something like, "What does it do?" The salesperson then begins describing that feature and is no longer concentrating on qualifying.

Ask questions that your customers can answer. Rephrase your questions so that the customer understands what you are talking about. Rather than asking if he would like a specific feature, state the benefit of that feature and ask if that is something that would interest him. If he has a good working knowledge of the product he is looking to buy and is already familiar with the jargon and technical terms related to it, you may find this approach unnecessary. How do you know if the person standing in front of you has this knowledge? Ask! "What features were you looking for in a . . . ?" If he possesses any knowledge about the product he will name several features in response.

As noted, most salespeople ask the wrong questions— closed-ended. These questions only require a yes or no response or one or two words:

- "Do you want this?"
- "Is this something you'd be interested in?"

- "We have some models that come with . . . . Is that something you'd like?"
- "Our new ones have . . . . Would you like that?"

Although closed-ended questions are useful in gathering information, they don't provide the opportunity for customers to express themselves fully. Closed-ended questions cut straight to the point. They give us the information we need and allow us to quickly identify what the customer wants. Asking this kind of question means that we can move quickly through the sales process. At the same time, these questions do absolutely nothing toward our building any kind of sound relationship with our customer.

As a rule, avoid questions that start like these:

- Are you?
- Do you?
- Will you?
- Would you?
- Have you?
- Is this?

Instead, ask questions that begin with "Who," "What," "Where," "When," "Why," and "How." These open-ended questions require the other person to answer with more than one or two words. They encourage her to give us more information. For example, "What were you looking for in a . . . ?" naturally prompts the customer to give us feedback.

Asking open-ended questions is more difficult than most salespeople realize. You have to think carefully before you ask. You have to change your old habits and techniques. To become skilled at posing such questions, you need to practise.

Exercise

This will help get you started. In your action planner, change each of the following closed-ended questions to an open-ended one.

- Will you be using this product at home?
- Are you interested in this feature?
- Will you be the only one using this item?
- Have you been shopping for this product very long?
- Is this the only store you've been into?
- Do you want your product to do this?
- Where will you be using this? At the office?

Take a moment and compare your responses with the ones listed below.

- Closed-ended: Will you be using this product at home?
- *Open-ended: Where will you be using this product?*

- Closed-ended: Are you interested in this feature?
- *Open-ended: What features are you interested in?*

- Closed-ended: Will you be the only one using this item?
- *Open-ended: Who else will be using this item?*

- Closed-ended: Have you been shopping for this product very long?
- *Open-ended: How long have you been shopping for this product?*

- Closed-ended: Is this the only store you've been into?
- *Open-ended: What other stores have you been into? or Where else have you been?*

- Closed-ended: Do you want your product to do this?
- *Open-ended: What do you want this product to do?*

- Closed-ended: Where will you be using this? At the office?
- *Open-ended: Where will you be using this?*

Your responses may vary from the ones recorded above. That's okay, as long as they begin with "the five W's" or "How" and typically would not be answered with a yes, no, or other one-or two-word replies.

Learning to ask open-ended questions is an acquired skill. You will probably find doing so difficult at first. Most of us tend to ask closed-ended questions in our casual everyday conversations. For example, "What plans do you have tonight? Going to a movie? A bar?"

Here is a list of open-ended questions to help you identify your customers' needs.

- Why are you buying a . . . ?
- Tell me how you use your . . . in a typical week.
- How will you be using your . . . ?
- What are you looking for in a . . . ?
- What features are you interested in?
- Why are those features important to you?
- Who else is involved in this decision?
- How do you plan to use your . . . ?
- What made you decide to visit our store?
- How long have you been shopping?

These questions will give the customer a greater chance to let you know what she is looking for, which will help put her at greater ease with you. Take a moment and in your action planner write down 10 or so other questions you could ask that are specific to your business.

One excuse salespeople give about asking open-ended questions is that the customer can respond with anything at all. Since an open-ended question is not a direct one, it does not—cannot—extract a specific piece of information. You might not be exactly sure where the discussion will end up. You might fear that you will lose control.

Let's look at this point from a slightly different perspective. If you have ever watched *Larry King Live* you will have noticed that his research team has done its homework. Mr. King has made himself very familiar with the information. He listens to the way his guest responds and then asks a question that is pertinent or relevant to the guest's last comment. He does not restrict himself to a list of scripted questions.

Almost every salesperson in the world could learn from his approach! He allows his guest to dictate where the flow of conversation goes while at the same time maintaining control of the entire process. Accordingly, guests on his show reveal information that many other interviewers could never coax out of them. How? He asks quality questions. He allows his guests to talk. He makes his guest feel as if she is the most important person in the world at that moment. He listens.

For the next week I want you to concentrate on asking some of these questions to gain more information from your customer. Notice how people respond to you. Pay attention to the information you will gather. Before we move on there is one last comment I'd like to make about questioning. Be careful not to end a question with a trailer. A trailer is a word that leaves another option available to the person questioned. Here are a couple of typical trailers: "Did you find everything you need or . . . ?" and "Are you interested in this feature or . . . ?"

Also, beware of inadvertantly turning an open-ended question into a closed-ended one. "Where will you be using this product? At the home? Office?" By adding "At the home? Office?" this question was turned into a closed-ended one.

Once you ask your customer a question, stop talking! Give her a chance to answer you.

Can I Ever Ask Closed-Ended Questions?

Yes, when you're dealing with a closed customer, also known as a low responder. These individuals tend to respond with a one- or two-word answer no matter what you ask them. If you ask how they will be using the product they will grunt, "Dunno." As you persevere with your open-ended questions, they doggedly continue to give you one- or two-word answers, which indicates that they do not want to be actively engaged in the sales process.

When you encounter this type of customer—and you will—switch your style of questioning. Shift to closed-ended questions. This will allow you to gather the information you need to serve this kind of customer. In this situation, your goal adjusts accordingly to gathering enough information to help this customer make her own educated decision.

Here is a rule of thumb: Use open-ended questions for open or responsive customers and closed-ended questions for closed or unresponsive customers. Not all potential customers will open up automatically when you begin asking them questions. In all cases, however, you want to give them time to become comfortable with you, the store, and the sales process.

What's Your Budget?

Avoid asking about the customer's budget concerns unless you sell items that range widely in price. I suggest this for three reasons:

1. Most customers will deliberately give you a figure lower than their actual budgets when asked such a general question because other salespeople have taken advantage of them in the past when they have done so. Think in particular of the car dealer who steered you to a car that fit your budget, then tried to up-sell additional features, options, extended warranties to you. Before you knew it, you had exceeded your original budget by hundreds, sometimes even thousands, of dollars.

2. By asking a customer budget questions, you could also be locking yourself into a particular price range. For example, if I am looking for new luggage and I tell you, the salesperson, I am looking for an inexpensive set, you will likely

show me the cheapest set you have in stock. What does "inexpensive" actually mean? To me, it could be anything under $800. For someone else, it may be the set that retails for $200. Don't jump to assumptions before gathering the information you need in order to proceed.

3. The third reason for avoiding the budget question is that you want to qualify your customer based on his needs. If he has a definite amount of money available for this purchase, he will tell you. Several years ago I needed a new suit. On a whim I ventured into Harry Rosen, a high-end menswear store. A sales associate greeted me and enquired why I had come to the store. When I told him I was in the market for a suit he said, "I'd like to ask you a few questions so I can determine what would be best for you." After a few minutes he directed me to a specific style. Based on the information he had gathered from me, he selected a suit that best met my needs rather than focusing on how much I planned to spend. Although I did have a certain budget in mind, I was also willing to spend more if the situation demanded it.

The Importance of Product Knowledge

The salesperson at Harry Rosen found out on what occasions I would wear my suit and then determined which one would best serve my needs as I outlined them. He reconfirmed all the qualifying questions he had asked me and then showed me how the particular suit he had selected would meet those requirements. He was able to do this because a) he knew my needs and b) he knew his products.

Here's an example of the opposite kind of sales service. At the time I was flying about 80,000 miles a year. I went shopping for a new garment bag, intending to find something very durable. I was examining several different bags in a store when I heard a voice behind me ask if I needed assistance. I turned around and faced a 17-year-old clerk. I explained my situation and she immediately held up a bag from the rack and said,

"This one looks nice." Needless to say, her lack of knowledge of the product and her inability to listen to and comprehend what I had told her influenced my buying decision. I didn't buy from that store.

- A true professional knows his products so well that he can explain a complex topic, product, or service in terms that a six-year-old can understand.
- A true professional studies and learns as much about her products as possible.
- A true professional speaks in lay terms, not jargon.

Product knowledge can be very difficult to obtain. Depending on what you are selling, you may find it next to impossible to gather all the knowledge you need to perform your job as smoothly as you would like. You don't have to know everything about every item you sell, but the more you know, the more your customers will respect you. They do expect you to have at least a good basic understanding of most of the products you sell.

Take the time to learn about the items you sell. Learn their different features and benefits. Understand how each feature and benefit fits in with the actual use of the product. Learn what distinguishes one item from another. Know your step-up and step-down models (the items priced immediately higher and lower), if appropriate. Demonstrate to your customer what makes you different from your competitors.

Hidden Issues

A concept often discussed in literature regarding sales negotiation is the Iceberg Theory. This states that in every negotiation only 10 to 20 percent of the information you require to achieve a win-win outcome is visible or apparent. A customer's hidden issues are concerns that will remain unstated unless the salesperson asks the customer a direct question.

To return to my earlier example, when my wife and I were looking for a washer and dryer we initially considered buying a particular brand of appliances. We had seen the advertising for them and believed they offered good value for the money. However, before we actually went shopping, a family member warned us that brand no longer gave as much priority to their products' quality as they had in the past. As our relative owned that brand's products herself, we considered her statement valid. When we went shopping we had this opinion in our minds, and although we never did ask a salesperson for validation or clarification, the comment influenced our final buying decision. Not one salesperson asked what we were looking for in a washer and dryer. To this day we don't know whether the information our relative gave us was accurate.

Your customers will have hidden issues and ideas that will influence the outcome of your sales to them. Your goal is to uncover these hidden issues. Obviously you cannot ask, "So do you have any hidden issues you'd like to discuss?" Instead, engage your customers in a discussion. Ask them open-ended questions such as,

- "Where else have you been?"
- "What have you seen so far?"
- "What has been your experience with this item?"
- "What did you like/dislike about . . . ?"
- "What have you heard about . . . ?"
- "What would you like to change from your existing situation?"
- "What was your experience at XYZ store?"

These questions will encourage your customers to share their thoughts, concerns, and feelings with you. If you listen closely to their responses, you should gain information pertaining to their hidden issues as well. Of course you will have to read between some lines and make a few assumptions. Armed with these, clarify your understanding of what your would-be customers are telling you:

- "It sounds as though you've had some challenges there."
- "It looks to me as if ABC store did not resolve your concern to your satisfaction."
- "From what you've told me, this seems to be a major concern for you."
- "I get the feeling that . . . "

Clarifying in this manner shows your customers that you have been paying attention to them. It will foster their trust in you and encourage them to trust you to find the product they are seeking. Don't start telling what you can do or how you compare favourably to your competitors. Instead, file this information away for later.

As noted earlier, many salespeople feel that asking all these questions puts the customer in control of the sale. They feel this way because they are not doing most of the talking themselves. However, the reverse is actually true. The person with the most information will control the agenda. As long as you are asking good questions you will be gaining information that keeps you in the driver's seat and driving in the direction you want to go— toward closing the sale. If the customers are the ones asking all the questions, they are the ones collecting the information and driving the car. Are you likely to end up where *you* want to be if you're not the one at the wheel?

Active Listening

Asking all the questions in the world will do no good if you don't listen to what the customers say in their answers. Part of establishing relationships with your customers is to listen actively to them. We all know that this is important; in the real world acting on this knowledge is often easier said than done. We face an array of barriers that prevents us from listening actively and effectively:

- interruptions from other customers
- interruptions from co-workers
- telephones ringing
- concerns about store security
- music playing in the store
- other people talking around you
- feeling overwhelmed by the number of customers in the store
- the way people are dressed
- being tired, sick, hungover, or bored
- knowing the store closes in a few minutes
- having other work to do
- feeling uninterested
- beginning to plan a response before the customer finishes answering your questions
- other customers waiting for you

You can overcome most of the items on this list with one simple technique: focus. If we focus on our customers, the ones who ultimately pay our salaries, then we *will* hear what they say. We *will* understand what they are looking for. We *will* build rapport with them. We *will* set ourselves apart from our competitors. To do this well, we need to employ a variety of active listening techniques, both verbal and non-verbal.

Verbal listening involves using the following five techniques:

1. Encourage the customer to continue by using prompters, such as "I see," "go on," "tell me more," "uh-huh."

2. Empathize with the customer to show that you understand, appreciate or respect their perspectives, opinions, or points of view. "I understand how you feel," "I appreciate your concern," "If that happened to me, I'd feel the same way."

3. Probe with more questions to follow up or clarify a customer's response to a previous question: "What other features would you find useful?"

4. Pause before you respond.

5. Summarize what you think you heard the customer saying in order to confirm that you get her point. "So if I understand you correctly, this is what you're looking for in a . . . ? Is that right?"

Each of these techniques accomplishes a different goal. Encouraging customers to talk enables you to gather more information and at the same helps your customers become more comfortable. Empathizing demonstrates to your customers that you understand what it feels like to be in their position. Probing helps you draw out more information that you might not otherwise have learned. Pausing before you respond to what they tell you gives you a moment to digest that information and reflect about what you are going to say. This can encourage a customer to continue talking, feeding you even more information. Summarizing shows that you have listened to your customer.

Non-verbal listening uses your eyes, face, and body to reflect your attention to, and your interest in, what the customer is saying.

• Make eye contact with the customer.

• Make responsive facial expressions such as frowning and smiling.

• Show attentiveness through body positioning and movement (leaning forward slightly, nodding or shaking your head, gesturing).

As we discussed in Chapter Two, body language is a powerful tool when used in conjunction with the appropriate words and proper tone of voice. If you want your customers to be interested in what you tell them about your product, you must show that you are interested in them first.

Over the years I have dealt with many sales professionals. The people who have impressed me the most were the ones who took a genuine interest in other people. These people seldom told their customers outright that they were better than their competition; they demonstrated it. They sought out the opportunity to create a specific relationship with each customer. They worked constantly at learning more about their customers. You too can develop this skill if you choose to. It takes effort. It takes time. Most importantly, it takes discipline.

Summarizing

Once you have asked the right questions, listened to your customer's response, and fully understood what he is looking for, you should verbally summarize this information to him aloud:

- **"From what you have told me, here's what you are looking for in a washer. You want an extra-large capacity, an alarm to indicate the end of the cycle, and . . . . Is that right?"**
- **"So based on what you have said, these are the most important features for you. You would like . . . . Would that be accurate?"**

This last step in the qualifying process is an important one. It shows that you've listened to your customer. It helps him confirm what he is looking for. If you have accidentally missed anything important, the customer will generally speak up and say, "Oh, I also want . . . " Summarizing also helps you determine if you have qualified the customer thoroughly. Your goal is to have enough information to make showing him more than one or two models unnecessary. If more than two products fit the requirements that the customer has outlined, ask at least one more question to eliminate one product. Once the customer has confirmed that you have an accurate understanding of his needs, you can then move to the next step in the process—the product presentation.

Stop, ask, and listen. Show you operate differently from your competition. Be different. Don't tell people that you are better than the business down the street; *show* them that difference. People believe what they see more than what they hear.

Sample Qualifying Conversations with Customers

Electronics Retailer

Salesperson: Hi, welcome to Ed's Electronics. What brings you in to our store today?

Customer: I'm just looking around.

Salesperson: That's good to hear. You'll be happy to know that the government hasn't found a way to tax that yet. (Pause.) What are you most interested in looking at?

Customer: Well, I'm considering buying a camcorder.

Salesperson: Great! We have lots to choose from. Do you mind if I ask you a few questions? That way I'll be able to point you in the right direction.

Customer: Yeah, I guess.

Salesperson: First of all, why are you interested in buying a camcorder?

Customer: My wife and I are having our first baby and we want to record all the special moments.

Salesperson: Oh that's great! I meet a lot of parents who do the same thing. When are you expecting?

Customer: Sometime in the next two weeks.

Salesperson: You must be getting excited. Do you mind if I ask where your wife is, since I assume you're making this purchase together.

Customer: Well, I'm doing the research and then we'll make the final decision together.

Salesperson: What other stores have you been to so far?

Customer: Carl's Candid Camera shop and Bombastic Bob's.

Salesperson: What was your experience there?

Customer: Not bad. They didn't seem to know much about the product, though, and it was difficult to get help.

Salesperson: That's too bad. Fortunately, we have several people who are very knowledgeable on cameras. Did you see anything that caught your attention?

Customer: They showed me quite a few cameras. Some had a side-viewing screen but I don't remember everything. They all looked pretty much the same to me.

Salesperson: What type of features would you like to have on your camera?

Customer: I'm not really sure. I've never owned one before. What do they come with?

Salesperson: They come with a wide variety of features. Tell me, in what conditions do you think you'll be using the camera?

Customer: Probably at home mostly. We'll likely take pictures at family functions, Christmas, birthdays, that sort of thing.

Salesperson: Okay, that's pretty standard. Are you looking to create special effects or titles?

Customer: Maybe. It depends on how expensive or difficult it is to use a feature like that.

Salesperson: Well, it varies. I'll you show you something in a few minutes that you might find interesting. In what other circumstances do you think you'll use the camera?

Customer: I don't really know. I think we'll just use it to film the baby. (Pause.) I want something easy to use. I'm not really a technical person with electronics.

Salesperson: No problem. The technology today makes it pretty easy to record great shots easily. Who do you know who currently owns a camera?

Customer: My brother has one. I've used it a couple of times and it's fairly easy to operate. He's got a feature that stabilizes the picture even when he's shooting from a moving vehicle. Also, he can hook it up to his computer and edit the stuff he's filmed. He often emails me still shots.

Salesperson: It's amazing what technology can do for you now. We have several cameras that will allow you to do that. (Pause.) So what you've told me so far is that you'll be using the camera primarily to take footage of your new baby. You might enjoy creating special effects and titles and you'd like a side-viewing screen. You also sound interested in being able to edit on your computer and email specific shots to family members at some point. Is that right?

Customer: Yeah, I think so.

Salesperson: Let me show you a model that will fit these needs perfectly.

Carpet Dealer

Salesperson: Welcome to Caz's Carpet's. What brings you into our store today?

Customer: We're looking for new carpet.

Salesperson: Great! Do you mind if I ask you a few questions? That way I'll be able to show you some samples that will fit your needs.

Customer: Sure.

Salesperson: First all of, where in your house are you placing the carpet?

Customer: In our home office.

Salesperson: Would you mind telling me about that room?

Customer: Well, it's about 12 by 14. The carpet we currently have is wearing pretty thin. I think it must be at least 10 or 12 years old. Anyway, it's kind of a dirty brown colour and we're looking for something different to brighten up the room.

Salesperson: That makes sense. What colour did you have in mind?

Customer: I think something in a medium to dark blue. The walls are a light blue and the furniture is mostly black.

Salesperson: How much time do you spend in that room in a typical day?

Customer: Anywhere from 4 to 10 hours. It depends how much work we have to do.

Salesperson: What type of business are you in?

Customer: My wife and I create marketing plans for independent business owners.

Salesperson: That sounds interesting. How long have you been involved in that?

Customer: Just over two years now.

Salesperson: How has business been?

Customer: Overall it's been pretty good. Some months it's really busy and other times it can be pretty quiet. Generally speaking, it stays fairly steady.

Salesperson: Great. I know the first couple of years of running a home-based business can be challenging. (Pause.) What thickness of pile were you considering for this carpet?

Customer: I think something with a medium thickness. I'd like to have something a bit thicker than our living and dining room carpet but not as plush as what's in our bedroom.

Salesperson: Okay. A couple of more questions. Who were you planning to have install the carpet?

Customer: Whoever we buy it from. We don't have time to do that.

Salesperson: I can certainly see why. I would imagine that your primary focus is running your business. What type of time frame were you considering?

Customer: Sometime in the next few weeks. We're not in a real rush, but I don't want to wait too long, either.

Salesperson: All right. Let me do a quick recap here. You're looking for carpet for your home office, which is about 12 by 14. You would like medium to dark blue with a medium pile. You'll want the dealer to install it and you're looking to make this purchase sometime in the next couple of weeks. Have I got everything?

Customer: It sounds like it.

Salesperson: Good. Let me show you a carpet that is very popular for home offices.

Car Dealer

Salesperson: Welcome to Quality Cars. What brings you to our lot today?

Customer: Just looking.

Salesperson: Great! We have lots to see. If you don't mind me asking, what specifically were you looking for?

Customer: A sports utility or a van.

Salesperson: Okay. What are you currently driving?

Customer: We have a Ford Tempo.

Salesperson: What's prompting you to look for another vehicle?

Customer: My husband and I need a second car. He's working longer hours and I need to take my kids to their sporting events. Also, it's too difficult to pack everything into the car.

Salesperson: I can certainly understand that. Many parents are finding the same thing. How many kids do you have?

Customer: We have three. Two boys and a girl.

Salesperson: That must keep you busy. You mentioned they're involved in sports?

Customer: Yes, my two boys play hockey and basketball. My daughter plays soccer and also takes gymnastics.

Salesperson: How long have they been involved in sports?

Customer: A few years now. This is the first year that they have all been taking two things each, though. At least it keeps them occupied and out of trouble. Coordinating the driving schedule can be a challenge.

Salesperson: I'll bet. Tell me, what have you and your husband discussed so far?

Customer: We're looking for something safe. Since I'm using it mostly to drive my children around I'm concerned about safety.

Salesperson: That's understandable. I'd feel the same way if I had children. What else is important to you?

Customer: I'm looking for something with good gas mileage. Most of my driving is in the city, so I know the mileage won't be that good, but I'm also concerned about the additional expense.

Salesperson: That makes sense. What other specific features were you interested in?

Customer: I saw some vans on the Internet that came with a built-in TV/VCR. I'd like one of those. I want air conditioning and it must be an automatic. Plus, the seats must be easy to remove so we can pack the hockey gear.

Salesperson: Sure. It sounds like you've done some homework. Do you mind if I ask where else you've looked so far?

Customer: This is the first place. I've done some research on the Internet, though.

Salesperson: The Internet can be a great place to get information. I notice your husband isn't with you. When do the two of you plan to shop together?

Customer: I'll bring him when we're ready to make a final decision.

Salesperson: Good idea. What's your deadline for buying this vehicle?

Customer: We don't really have one. We plan to buy when we find a van that meets all of our needs.

Salesperson: Let me take a moment and recap our discussion. You're looking for a new van with lots of safety features to protect your kids. You would prefer a model with good gas mileage, particularly in the city. You want a TV/VCR, air conditioning, and you want to be able to remove the seats easily. Is that everything?

Customer: I think so. Oh, if possible I also want a GPS [global positioning satellite] system. I don't like reading maps and I've heard that the new GPS systems are pretty good.

Salesperson: They are. Let me show you a couple of styles of vans that I think you'll like.

Qualifying Questions

Here is a summary of effective qualifying questions that were presented in this chapter.

1. What are you looking for in a . . . ?
2. What features interest you?
3. Why are those features important to you?
4. What brings you into our store today?
5. Who else is part of the buying process?
6. Who else is involved in this decision?
7. How long have you been shopping?
8. What else have you seen?
9. Where else have you been?
10. What was your experience at . . . ?
11. What do/did you like or dislike about your previous unit/set?
12. What comments do you have about what you've seen so far?
13. What deadlines are you up against?
14. When are you looking to make this purchase?
15. Why are you buying a . . . ?
16. How do you plan to use your . . . ?
17. Tell me how you use your . . . in a typical week?
18. What would you change in your present situation?

Rapport-Building Questions

1. What kind of car do you drive?

2. How do you like it?

3. How old are your children?

4. What are their names?

5. Where are you going on your vacation?

6. How was your vacation?

7. Tell me about your . . . .

8. What type of work do you do?

9. How long have you been doing that?

10. What do you enjoy most about it?

11. How did you become involved in that line of work?

12. What sports interest you?

13. What kind of hobbies do you enjoy?

Additional questions for specific types of retail environments are listed in Appendix 1.

Summary

- Invest the appropriate amount of time in determining the needs and wants of your customers.

- Every customer has two types of needs, logical and emotional. Logical needs pertain directly to the product features; emotional needs revolve around our feelings. Focus on learning your customers' emotional needs, as they are the motivating factors in their purchase decision.

- Control the sale by asking questions. The person who asks the questions is in control. If the customer is asking all the questions, he or she will direct the sale.

- When people ask "What's your best price?" respond with one of these comments:

  1. "My best price is (quote full retail). Would you mind if I asked you a few questions to determine if this is the right model for you?"

  2. "My best price is (quote full retail). It appears that you've been shopping around. Do you mind if I ask what you've seen?"

  3. "My best price is (quote full retail). You seem to know what you're looking for. How did you decide this model is the right one for you?"

- Establish rapport with your customers by asking them personal questions in a manner that is non-threatening. Allow them plenty of time to answer.

- You will prevent later objections by building rapport with your customers at the outset of the sales interaction.

- Learn to ask open-ended questions beginning with "What," "Who," "Where," "Why," "When," "How."

- Avoid closed-ended questions unless dealing with a very unresponsive person. Closed-ended questions begin with, "Are you . . . ?" "Do you . . . ?" "Will you . . . ?" "Have you . . . ?" "Would you . . . ?" "Will you . . . ?" "Is this . . . ?"

- Ask questions that will encourage your customers to share their feelings and disclose hidden issues. Hidden issues always influence the outcome of the sale. Learn what may prevent your customer from making the purchasing decision.

- Really listen to your customer. Be aware of the barriers to active listening and concentrate on overcoming them. Listen for cues and clues.

- Summarize what your customer has told you before you start your presentation.

Action Plan

In your action planner, answer these questions:

1. What did you learn in this chapter?
2. How does this apply to what you do?
3. What will you do differently starting today?

Explaining the Product

**"People don't care how much you know until they know
how much you care."**

If you want to set yourself apart from your competition, learn how to deliver an effective presentation to your customers. My experience as a consumer and sales trainer has taught me that most salespeople have a very unfocused approach to their presentations—if they even do one. They ramble on and on, talking aimlessly about every feature the product has to offer. Or they stand around and wait until the customer asks a question before providing the information. Worse still are the salespeople who have no knowledge or understanding of their product, its features, or how it operates, and try to bluff their way through the presentation.

This chapter discusses how you can develop a presentation that will knock the socks off your customer's feet. We will look at some of the most common mistakes made by salespeople during their presentation. We will examine some words you can use to enhance your presentation. We will look at how you can involve your customers and how to keep them interested. We will also review the difference your enthusiasm can make. You will learn to incorporate additional tools into your presentation to help you differentiate yourself from your competitors.

Common Presentation Mistakes

Salespeople make a variety of mistakes during their presentation of their product or service. These are:

1. They forget the purpose of the presentation.

2. They do not adapt their presentation.

3. They fail to engage the customer.

4. They use too much jargon.

5. They talk too fast or too much.

6. They give the customer too much information.

7. They make elaborate claims about their product or service.

8. They lack enthusiasm.

9. They lack product knowledge.

10. They discuss features instead of benefits.

11. They allow themselves to become distracted.

Mistake #1—They forget the purpose of the presentation.

The purpose of the presentation is to show your customer how your product or service fits their specific needs. It is for their benefit, not yours. It is not the time for you to brag about how good or knowledgeable or experienced you are. Your customers don't care about that. They want to know how your particular product or service will help them.

Years ago, I worked in the hospitality industry. In one organization I eventually began conducting the in-house training program for new franchisees. After receiving positive feedback from a number of participants, I started one session by telling the franchisees how good the program was, that I was very competent, and how much they would learn with me. My intent was not to brag but to allay any concerns about the value of the program. Needless to say my message was not interpreted this way and it didn't take long for one owner to track down my boss and complain about my behaviour. After my boss kicked away the pedestal I was sitting on, he explained that I didn't have to tell the group I was capable of delivering the program. Instead, he told me to focus on conducting the program to the best of my ability and the participants would see that they were in good hands. This valuable lesson has remained with me to this day.

You need to be able to speak intelligently about your product or service. You must be able to discuss how certain features will help your customer. But you should not spend much time telling your customer about aspects of your product or service that have no relevance to their specific situation. Remember, the purpose of the presentation is to help the customer make a decision, not for you to brag about your skill or knowledge.

Mistake #2—They do not adapt their presentation.

This is one of the biggest mistakes a sales professional can make. Every single person you interact with is different from the previous person you spoke to. Even if both are seeking to buy the same item, they will have different reasons for doing so. Therefore, it is critical that you adapt your presentation to address each person's specific needs and wants. If you launch into a canned or rehearsed presentation after investing time asking the customer about their needs, you will quickly lose credibility.

I once worked for a large organization and was tasked with heading up an e-learning initiative. This meant I needed to meet with vendors of distance learning products. The salesperson from one company asked me a few questions about my business while powering up his notebook. As he walked through his PowerPoint slides, it became obvious this was a standard presentation. As a result, none of my questions or concerns was addressed. I voiced my displeasure and he requested permission to log onto his website so he could show me how my questions would be answered.

This, too, resulted in a canned presentation. Now, after spending over 30 minutes with him and still not receiving satisfactory answers, I ended the meeting.

Compare this to the following encounter I experienced with a well-known training company a few weeks later. After researching a variety of activities, I met with their account manager. I asked him about a specific activity that appealed to me but instead of jumping into a presentation about this product, he asked me several questions about my objectives, business challenges, and learning strategies. After gathering this information, he recommended a different activity and during his discussion he referred to specific comments I had stated earlier. Asking me appropriate questions gave him the information he needed to ensure his presentation addressed my particular situation.

Rather than discuss all the features of the product, first demonstrate the ones that the customer cited as important to her. Use the information you gathered in the previous step constructively. Maximize your efforts by working smarter.

For example, "Mrs. Jones, you mentioned that you're looking for a loveseat with a hideaway bed that moves easily in the chair. This particular model has just that. Let me show you how easy it is to pull out the bed and then put it back again." Once you have shown the customer a specific feature, allow her to experiment with it. Give her time and space to see how that particular feature works.

I recall buying broadloom for our house. The salesman in the first store was very knowledgeable and he made no bones about telling me that. He told me that he had been in the business for more than 20 years, that he was the company's troubleshooter and that he went from store to store helping them out. Blah, blah, blah. He kept talking about himself instead of focusing on my needs. On top of the fact that he didn't address my concerns, he also failed to engage me in the buying process.

Mistake #3—They fail to engage the customer.

I eventually asked this salesperson about underpadding and he launched into a 10-minute lecture on the differences between the three grades of underpadding. Because I am not in the carpet business, I promptly forgot everything he told me as soon as I left the store.

The next store, however, was a different story. The salesman there encouraged me to remove my shoes while he placed a swatch of broadloom on the three samples of underpadding. He then told me to stand on each sample, allowing me to feel what it would be like in my house, under my feet. While I was experiencing the sensation of the carpet under my feet, he explained a few of the key differences between each piece of underpadding. His presentation took a total of 90 seconds and had a far greater impact. He actively engaged me in the presentation and made it easy for me to understand and absorb the information he was sharing.

Involving the customer in the demonstration will enhance her shopping experience. If you sell beds, encourage people to remove their shoes and lie down on the bed in the same position they do at home. Make sure you have a variety of pillows available. Allow people to pull covers up over themselves—in other words, put sheets on the beds! If you sell electronics, hand them the remote control. Explain a feature, show them how it works, then allow them to operate it. Make them more than passive bystanders—get that remote in their hands! If you sell cars, encourage them to take a test drive. As a customer myself, I cannot stand listening to a car salesperson while he drones on about the engine size, power, and other related details. I want to feel the car as it accelerates. I want to see how it handles around corners and on the highway. I want to hear how much road noise is evident. I want to touch it, feel it, experience it.

If you sell luggage, have customers hang the garment bag over their shoulder. If you sell jewelry tell them to try on the ring rather than holding it in their fingers. Don't force people to be passive bystanders. They are the ones spending the money and paying your salary. Give them a reason to buy from you instead of a competitor.

Again, the message—*show* your customers that you're different than your competition; don't tell them. Virtually every retailer claims to have great products at a great price. *Show* your customers what separates you from everyone else who sells similar items. You must give them compelling reasons to buy from you. You can go a long way toward achieving this goal by encouraging them to participate in your sales demonstration.

Mistake #4—They use too much jargon.

"The Ultra-deluxe Hyperfold 2000 is an awesome machine. It comes equipped with the patented Superglide sling arm, a pair of DXT mini boosters, and a Veltor load intensifier that will help you increase the magnitude of your velocity charged magnifiers."

Huh?

Every industry has terminology that is relevant to its products and services. Many salespeople baffle their customers by using words, phrases, or jargon that the customer is unfamiliar with. I've seen expressions of confusion on many a person's face while the salesperson describes the features of a certain item. The salesperson seems to think that the demonstration of her knowledge will help her customer recognize how smart she is. Here's a little secret: customers don't care how much you know. In fact, they don't care about you at all—not until they know how *you* care about *them*.

As you make your way through your presentation, make sure you speak in terms your customer understands. Avoid using company jargon or techno-babble unless you know the other person understands it. If you notice his eyes glazing over or he looks lost or confused, stop. Rephrase what you've just said in lay terms. Show you customer how much you care by using language he can understand. The most adept sales professionals can describe their product to an individual who lacks even a basic knowledge as well as to people who possess a comprehensive understanding.

A perfect example of this was a manager I once worked with in an electronics company. It was my second day on the job and Chris was explaining some fundamental concepts to me in a manner that helped make it easy for me to grasp. Later in the morning, a customer entered the store and began discussing his requirements for a home theatre system in what sounded like a foreign language. Recognizing that this individual was very well-informed, Chris immediately modified his approach and began speaking at the same level.

If you work in a specialized field (such as electronics, computer- or Internet-related, automobiles, advertising, or publishing), recognize that many of the people you deal with will not possess the insider knowledge that you do. Participants in my workshops tell me that they will ask a question like, "Do you understand?" during their presentation. This tends to be ineffective because most people will not admit they do not understand something. Instead, they will nod their head, smile, and respond positively. But, going through their mind is, "I have no idea what he means. I probably should but I don't want him to think I'm stupid. I'll figure it out later." I experienced this when I was planning my website. Both my web designer and host used terminology that meant nothing to me and I was reluctant to ask for clarification.

Again, make it easy for people to do business with you by learning how to explain your product or service in terms they can easily understand.

Mistake # 5—They talk too fast or too much.

It is not uncommon to see salespeople dominate the discussion. Some feel that telling is selling; others believe they need to talk more to control the sale; others think they have to speak faster in order to discuss everything about the product.

People tend to speak more rapidly when they are nervous and salespeople experience anxiety during the sales process. Tension is often caused because the salesperson is too focused on closing the sale. He may be experiencing a slow month; a co-worker might be having a better month. His boss could be pushing for more sales, or another salesperson may have just closed a major sale. These external forces create additional pressure to close the sale and cause him to speak faster.

In situations such as this, customers will have a difficult time keeping up so they will naturally begin to lose interest.

This often causes the salesperson to speed up his delivery even more to ensure the customer hears everything about the product or service.

A few years ago I spoke to a salesperson from a local training firm who was interested in selling me a training game. Our initial telephone conversation lasted twice as long as it should have because this individual spent far too much time talking. Even as a skilled workshop leader, it was difficult for me to find an appropriate time to interject. However, I was intrigued by the product and agreed to meet with him. This time I set a deadline for our conversation so he wouldn't ramble on so long.

Mistake #6—Giving the customer too much information.

Salespeople often feel compelled to tell the customer everything there is to know about their product or service. What they fail to remember is that most customers don't want all that information. They want to know what is relevant to their specific situation. If you discuss elements of your product that have little or no relevance for your customers, they will quickly tune you out. When you give them too much information, you actually make it more difficult for them to make a decision. This is particularly true with complex products.

It is important to keep your presentations focused. Most presentations lack direction. They have no beginning or structured end. The salesperson just starts talking . . . and talking . . . and talking . . . and talking. Sometimes the information she reveals is relevant to the customer's needs; often it is not.

The most effective way of showing customers that you care is to concentrate your presentation on their specific needs. This is another reason I suggest that you summarize your understanding of their needs before you begin. Rather than discuss all the features of the product, first demonstrate the ones that the customer cited as being important. Use the information you gathered in the previous step constructively. Maximize your efforts by working smarter.

Mistake #7—Making elaborate claims about your product or service.

Most people have been exposed to numerous infomercials on television. We have heard spokespeople make outlandish claims about their product. Naturally, this causes skepticism.

In their eagerness to close the sale, salespeople can get caught up in telling white lies or stretching the truth. The customer asks if the product will perform in a certain manner, and the salesperson responds in the affirmative before thinking through her answer. When the customer eventually discovers that the product does not perform as expected, he begins to doubt the word of other salespeople he interacts with.

Before you answer a customer's question make sure the response you give is accurate. This can be particularly challenging in an environment where the manager places undue pressure on the sales team to close more sales. I have heard countless stories of managers saying to their staff, "No one walks today. Do whatever it takes to close the sale." This message sends a strong signal to the team that underhanded techniques and strategies will be accepted. While you may close the sale by "fudging the truth" you will not develop customer loyalty. It doesn't take long for word to spread about companies who deliberately mislead their customers. Here is a fact: a dissatisfied customer will tell approximately 18 to 20 people about the experience. Those individuals will then tell an additional two to four people about the previous person's situation. That means up to 100 people can hear about a single negative experience.

When you do not know the answer, consult someone else, refer to a manual, or tell the customer that you simply do not know. Although customers may not like this last answer, they will respect you for saying so. I recommend you tell customers that you will find an answer and get back to them. Then make sure you do.

Mistake #8—Lacking enthusiasm.

Have you ever had to listen to a really boring lecture? I've endured many sales presentations that are not much better. If you don't get excited about what you are saying, how can you expect your customer to get enthused about making a purchase?

Present the product to your customer with passion. Be enthusiastic. Even though we all know enthusiasm is contagious, as a consumer I seldom hear much energy, excitement, or enthusiasm in a salesperson's voice. It is almost as if she is afraid that any enthusiasm will indicate she is too hungry for the sale. In fact, showing emotion and getting excited don't suggest a desperate salesperson; rushing through the sales process does.

Words Make a Difference

A few words can make a tremendous difference in the way a customer perceives your presentation. For example,

> "Oh, we're out of stock."
> "We can't get any until next month."
> "All we have left is this demo unit."
> "You can try getting it at one of our other stores."
> "We can order that, but it will take three to four weeks for delivery."

All these statements are negative. Consciously or not, the customer is influenced by that tone. Making your words positive can persuade your customer to decide to buy the product anyway:

> "We're completely sold out!"
> "They're selling so fast we can't keep them in stock!"
> "We have a display unit available right now."
> "Let me contact one of our other stores and see if they can help."
> "We can order that for you and have it in just three to four weeks."

By rephrasing a sentence with a few different words you have changed the entire message. Emphasize the right words with the appropriate tone of voice. The result is a positive message, one that encourages the customer to buy.

Pay close attention to the words your customers use when you are identifying *their* needs. Use their words when describing the product to them. For example, if the customer says he is looking for plush carpet, demonstrate your carpet by saying, "This carpet is very plush. Why not take off your shoes and see how it will feel in your home?" Using the same words your customer used will help him clearly identify with your presentation.

Selecting the correct approach is another important part of using the right words. In Chapter Four I discussed two kinds of needs: logical and emotional. As you uncover these needs, determine what type of presentation best suits each customer— a logical or an emotional one.

If your customer has expressed that logical needs are most important to him, focus on the features of the product. Use logic in your presentation.

Focus on the emotional value of making the purchase when the customers' needs are primarily psychological. Incorporate feelings and benefits during your presentation.

This approach will help you connect with your customer and, again, demonstrate how you differ from your competition.

Mistake #9—They lack product knowledge.

In the previous chapter, I mentioned how important product knowledge is to you in effectively qualifying a customer. It is also critical when it comes time to explain your product. Not every customer wants a detailed explanation of how every feature works. But for those who do, you need to be ready. The vast majority of products on the market require some form of technical knowledge in order to sell them properly. Obviously, the more items you sell and the more complicated they are, the more challenging this will be.

Retail consumers are more knowledgeable and have access to more information than ever before. Many consumers take advantage of the information available on the Internet and come into your store armed and prepared. This means you need to invest time learning as much about your products as possible. You need to be able to discuss your products with every type of customer you interact with. You must be able to answer questions that relate to how each product operates, the proper care and maintenance, warranty specifications, product features, and how similar items differ from each other. One of the quickest ways to lose credibility with a customer is to shrug your shoulders and say, "I don't know" when they ask you a question. If, for whatever reason, you don't know the answer, don't BS the customer. There is no faster way to lose credibility than to lie to a customer.

I am an avid runner and have completed two marathons and several half-marathons. I buy my shoes from one specific store because the company invests in helping their sales associates learn as much about their product offering as possible. They can answer my questions and always help me buy the style and type of shoe that is best for my needs.

The more expensive or technical your product, the more important product knowledge becomes. Invest the time learning as much about your products as possible. This investment will always pay dividends.

Mistake #10—They discuss features instead of benefits.

People buy benefits, not features. So part of the presentation process entails understanding the appropriate benefit for a specific feature. When you're pointing out a certain feature, ensure that you explain its benefit as well. The feature is "what it is" whereas the benefit is "what it means to the customer." For instance, "This running shoe has extra support in the arch, which means it will reduce the potential for knee pain. You mentioned that you run long distances on a regular basis. This shoe will reduce your leg and foot fatigue." Don't assume that customers will know what the benefit of a feature is. Tell them.

Exercise

In your action planner, list three products you sell. Then record their features and the appropriate benefits for each. Use the following process:

Product: _____

Feature: _____

which means, Benefit: _____

Linking the benefit of a specific feature to the product's actual use helps your customers clearly understand how that feature applies to them. For example, if you are discussing ABS brakes on a car, you could say, "If you're driving in a snowstorm and you have to stop suddenly, these brakes will not lock up, so you won't end up in an uncontrollable skid." Rather than simply stating, "This car has ABS brakes," you have now told the customer the benefit and how that will affect him in actual, everyday situations.

Mistake #11—They allow themselves to become distracted.

Retail is a dynamic environment. Sales associates are faced with a multitude of distractions:

- people entering and exiting the store
- deliveries
- the telephone ringing
- extra tasks or side duties that must be completed
- the physical appearance of people
- the number of customers in the store
- security issues
- interruptions by customers, co-workers or managers
- customers who talk too much or ramble
- crying children
- presentations being conducted by other sales associates
- volume level of the back/foreground music

- language barriers
- not enough employees to handle the traffic
- new or slower employees
- stock being misplaced
- disorganized store
- lack of store supplies

Some of these distractions are controllable. Others are not. However, it is important to recognize that they all distract sales associates from delivering a quality sales presentation.

The key strategy for you is to focus on your presentation. Remember, the purpose of the presentation is for the customer's benefit, not yours. Give each and every customer 100 percent of your attention. This requires focus and attention. But it makes a tremendous difference in how your customers perceive you and your company. Plus, it greatly influences their decision to buy from you versus someone else.

Painting Mental Pictures

"And for dessert, we have this incredible Bombastic Brownie that will electrify your tastebuds. We start with a fresh home-made brownie that's warmed up until it is piping hot. We add two scoops of rich French vanilla ice cream to it and then drizzle chocolate fudge over the top. Then we swirl fresh whipping cream over that and top it off with a bright-red maraschino cherry. It's only $4.95."

Are you drooling? Can't you visualize this luscious dessert in your mind? Compare that presentation with this one: "And for dessert, we have a brownie with ice cream. It's $4.95."

Experienced restaurant servers understand the importance of using descriptive words to enhance their dishes. You can also use this concept when talking about your products or services. Create mental images that correspond to your customers' psychological needs. Help them visualize the ways the product will enhance their lives, reduce stress, increase comfort, or make them more productive. Show them how simple it is to use, or how their friends will respond to their having it. Draw them into your presentation; get them excited about what you are selling.

Compare a high-quality training seminar to a university lecture. In the lecture you listen passively; at the seminar you participate actively. Which role do you enjoy the most?

Several years ago the movie *Just the Ticket* dramatized this concept. Andy Garcia plays a ticket hustler who desperately wants to date Andie McDowell. In one particular scene she agrees to have dinner with him if he can sell a big-screen television to a blue-collar worker. Garcia's character presents this TV to his customer with passion, emotion, and a variety of descriptive words and phrases. He captures the customer's attention and interest, and, ultimately, the customer decides to buy the system.

Exercise

Now it's your turn. In your downloadable action planner, list several products you sell in the store where you work. Then list at least six adjectives that best describe it. Feel free to use words from the list below:

Texture: soft, pliant, warm, cozy, hard, firm, cold, smooth, delicate, pliable, textured, rough, sharp, flexible, pointed, rounded, slick, fluffy, cool, light.

Sound: loud, bass, crisp, roar, booming, thundering, balanced, quiet, whisper silent, subtle, pitch, clarity, static-free, soft, clear, electric.

Appearance: bright, crisp, brilliant, soft, appealing, pleasing, vivid, sharp, reflective, detailed, vibrant.

Taste: rich, decadent, tasty, flavorful, moist, hot, cold, tangy, salty, sweet, spicy.

The next challenge is learning to use these words and phrases effectively. If you overuse adjectives, your presentation will not sound natural. If you use inappropriate words for the customer or product, you will lose credibility. If you use words that you are uncomfortable with, your customer will notice it. The trick is to gradually build up your repertoire and have at your disposal words and phrases that you can use in every situation.

Here is an example of the impact that mental imagery can have on the sales process. Six months after my wife and I bought our first home, we went shopping for a gas barbeque. During the entire winter I had created the mental image of standing on my back deck, cooking wonderful food for family and friends. I could almost smell the smoke from the flames and hear the sizzling of the steak on the grill. When we finally went shopping it was very easy for the salesperson to steer me to the high-end section because I could envision my family and friends oohing and aahing as I prepared them a feast fit for royalty.

That is why it is so important that you uncover your customer's psychological needs. Adapt your presentation to address these needs. In doing so, you will prove to your customer that you stand head and shoulders above your competition.

Another effective way of keeping your customers' interest is to tell them stories. As a keynote speaker, I have learned that most of us love a good story, particularly if we can see its relevance to our own lives. Draw on your own experience to generate a tale or anecdote and link it to your customer's situation. Use a variety of descriptive words to create a powerful mental image in your customer's mind.

Tools of the Trade

Imagine a carpenter showing up at a building site without a tape measure or saw. Would a professional hockey player arrive at the arena without his favourite stick? Can you see a musician coming into a recording studio and asking to borrow a guitar?

Each of these professionals has tools that are used in his or her trade. We sales professionals, too, should have a variety of tools at our fingertips when we begin a presentation. These will help us enhance our presentation and, eventually, close the sale.

I ventured into a high-end men's clothing store one weekend clad in jeans, a sweatshirt, and sneakers. I was looking for just a suit. The salesman who served me made sure I was fitted with a proper dress shirt, dress shoes and socks, a beautiful leather belt, and a gorgeous silk tie. He knew the value of utilizing the tools he had at his disposal to help me move toward a purchasing decision.

Exercise

In your action planner, identify as many as a dozen tools or props you can use to improve your presentation and set yourself apart from your competitors. Don't include pens, pencils, name tags, or business cards. These are a given that all sales professionals should carry with them at all times. Think of items that most salespeople would not normally use in their presentation. For example, if you sell computer products have printed sample sheets showing what each printer produces; CDs with sound, pictures, and graphics; and photos to demonstrate scanning quality.

Now consider how you will incorporate these tools into your existing presentation. It is not enough to have a tool or prop available—you must also determine how you will use it. Keep these items in an area in the store where you will have easy access to them at all times. Make these props part of every presentation you give to your customers.

Excellent presentations don't just happen. They require careful planning and preparation. They need thought. Avoid launching into a canned pitch regardless of how often you have talked about that particular item. Keep your presentation fresh; make it exciting and captivating. Give your customers a reason to return to you again and again.

Summary

- Keep the presentation focused on your customers' needs, particularly their emotional needs.
- Engage them actively in the process. Involve them by asking them to touch, feel, and experiment with the product.
- Ensure that your knowledge of the product is excellent. Don't BS people if you don't know something; find out the answer. Customers will respect your honesty.
- Remember that people buy benefits, not features. Always tell them the benefits of a specific feature.
- Speak in terms they can understand and relate to—logical or emotional.
- Paint mental pictures to enhance your presentation. Tell stories and use anecdotes.
- Be enthusiastic during your entire presentation. How can you expect your customer to get excited if you are not?
- Incorporate the use of props and tools into your presentations. Show that you're different from your competition.

Action Plan

In your action planner, answer these questions:

1. What did you learn in this chapter?
2. What will you now do differently during your next shift?
3. What challenges do you anticipate?
4. How will you overcome these challenges?

Solving Objections

"Objections do not have to be negative; in many cases they indicate a willingness to buy."

Objections are an inevitable aspect of selling. They don't have to be difficult or frustrating to deal with. Successful sales professionals consider objections a natural part of selling and have learned how to deal with them. If you follow the concepts discussed in Chapter Four, you will find most customers raise fewer objections in the first place. Assuming that you will inevitably face some objections, here are four steps that will help you overcome them more effectively.

1. **Empathize.** This means that you express your understanding of your customer's perspective in words. "I understand how you feel; this is a large investment."

2. **Ask for clarification.** Ensure that you fully understand exactly what her objection is. "Do you mind if I ask why you feel that way?"

3. **Seek permission.** This is also known as "bridging." You are asking the customer for permission to provide a solution. "Would it be okay if I explained some of the benefits of buying from our store?"

4. **Provide a solution.** Explain a solution that suits his specific situation.

Although this process appears long and drawn out when stated this way, step-by-step, it actually only takes a few moments. If you discipline yourself to use these four steps consistently, you will overcome more objections in less time.

What Is an Objection?

First, it is important to understand the difference between an objection and a condition of sale. You can always offer a solution for an objection. A condition of sale is a factor beyond your control. If a customer wants a red suitcase and all you sell are black ones, you will not likely close the sale no matter how hard you try. You simply don't have the product the customer is looking for. To her, the suitcase's colour is a condition of the sale. On the other hand, if the price exceeds the customer's budget you may be able to solve that objection in one of several ways—depending on where you work.

Second, a request for information is different from an objection. A question such as "Why should I buy from you?" is a question, not an objection. The customer who asks this question wants verification from you that buying from you is a good idea.

I will return to the washer and dryer purchase for a moment. My wife and I were concerned about buying a particular brand of washer. When the salesperson in the first store asked us what we were looking for, we told him and my wife responded with, "But not this brand." Although the salesperson treated this statement as an objection, it was actually a request for information. My wife wanted to know whether or not the information we had been given was accurate.

Many salespeople confuse these two obstacles and they waste precious time, effort, and energy stewing about things over which they have little or no control. A condition of sale is usually something customers need or want before they will go ahead and make their final purchase. Things like a particular style of product, colour, delivery, or payment terms.

An objection is a concern that remains unresolved in the customer's mind. Once you determine that you are dealing with an actual objection, learn to follow the four steps:

Step 1—Empathize

"I can appreciate why you'd feel that way." Many salespeople mentally empathize with their customers. Unfortunately, this is not enough. You need to express this aloud to your customers. Putting empathy into words shows your customers that you care, that you are on their side, that you understand, respect, or appreciate them. Empathy is a powerful tool. Most people want others to empathize with them and their situation. When I first began running I experienced shin splints. Shin splints are a very painful injury often caused by worn-out shoes. While I was replacing my shoes I began telling the sales associate about my injury so she could fully understand what I needed.

Empathy can be used very effectively in service issues. Consider the customer who is returning a defective product. He is often upset, angry, frustrated. When he begins his attack, our first reaction is to retaliate with a comment like, "I just sell them, I don't make them" or "Yeah, we get this model returned a lot." Such comments only fuel the customer's already heated emotions. It is more advantageous to empathize with him in a situation like this. "You have every right to be upset, I'd feel the same way too. Let me see what I can do to help."

Empathy helps diffuse the situation. It helps reduce the customer's hostility, and it helps you move toward a solution. A few years ago I received a parking ticket. On reading it carefully, I noticed that the street name was incorrectly recorded. I drove to the city finance office to discuss the error. When the clerk enquired whether I was disputing the ticket, I said yes. She responded, "If you want to dispute the ticket you'll have to show up in court." As I continued to question her, she kept repeating this. No matter what I said, she repeated the same thing over and over. Needless to say, my level of frustration escalated dramatically. Surely she could have told me, "I can appreciate your frustration, Mr. Robertson. Unfortunately, my hands are tied. In situations like this, it's your word against the parking officer's so the matter has to be handled in court." If she had said this along with offering some genuine empathy I would have paid the $10 fine and been on my way.

So . . . how does this apply to dealing with objections?

When a customer objects to something, she is handing you her problem. She is waiting for you to start overcoming the objection and, in most cases, that is what you do. The problem is that the customer may not be ready to accept your solution. Empathizing with her will help you create this state of mental readiness. You are demonstrating that you care about her and you are helping her build trust. You are demonstrating that you are on her side rather than opposing her.

There are many ways to phrase an expression of empathy:

- "I understand how you feel."
- "I appreciate your concern."
- "I respect your decision."
- "I see why you feel that way."
- "I've been there, so I know how you feel."
- "You're right—it is a major investment."
- "You're not alone; other people have said the same thing."
- "That's not the first time I've heard that."
- "I hear what you're saying."
- "I see what you mean."

Each of these statements demonstrates your understanding of the customer's perspective. You can adapt these statements to each customer you deal with and the specific objection he or she presents.

This step is more difficult for male sales associates to grasp than for their female counterparts. Women tend to be more empathetic in nature while men are more focused on solving the problem. Even though men may feel empathic in a given situation, they seldom verbalize it. Hundreds of sales training workshops have confirmed this. Therefore, for the male readers of this book, I will suggest you pay particular attention to this chapter and complete the exercises here.

Step 2—Ask for Clarification

Once you have empathized with your customer, immediately clarify his objection. Restate the objection back to the customer in your own words to ensure that you have correctly understood what his actual objection is.

I frequently hear two protests at this point. The first is, "I've heard all these objections before, so I know what they mean." Second, "People are going to think I'm talking down to them."

Let me first address the first concern. Objections such as "It's too expensive" can have several meanings:

- The customer does not see the value of the product or service.
- He cannot afford it.
- He has seen it cheaper somewhere else.
- He is comparing it to another brand.
- He is objecting as a negotiating tactic.
- He has not budgeted enough for it.
- His perception of the cost may be unrealistic.
- He is objecting as an excuse to leave the store without making the purchase.

At least eight different reasons behind one objection. How can you possibly offer the appropriate solution unless you know *exactly* what the customer means? If you take the time to fully comprehend what your customer actually means, you will be better equipped to deal with his objection.

It is important to be aware that the customers' first objection are seldom their real concern. In many cases you will need to empathize and clarify several times to uncover their true objections. Assuming you employ the appropriate tone of voice and body language you should be able to repeat this process three or four times. Here is an example:

You: So, would you like to go with that one?

Customer: I'd like to think about it.

You: *Empathize:* Sure, I can appreciate that. Many of my customers like to think about their purchase.

                Clarify: What is it that you'd like to think about?

Customer: I'm going to check with my wife.

You: *Empathize:* I think that's a smart idea. I usually consult with my wife when considering a large purchase.

                Clarify: What concerns do you think she might have?

Customer: I'm not sure she will like the colour.

You: *Empathize:* That's not uncommon; after all, she's not here with you to help make that decision.

                Clarify: So, if I understand you correctly, your primary concern has to do with the colour of this product, right?

Customer: Yeah, what happens if she doesn't like it? Can I exchange it?

In this situation the customer's true objection revolved around the return or exchange policy. However, the customer did not initially express that as his objection. Instead, he responded with "I'll think about it" which is one of the most common objections salespeople hear. And, in many cases, they respond by saying something such as, "No problem. Let me know if you have any questions." We hand them a business card and allow them to leave the store without fully understanding what concern was preventing them from making a decision. That is why this step in the objection-handling process is so important.

Clarifying is not...

- Clarifying does not mean asking, "Other than that, what's preventing you from making this purchase?"
- Clarifying does not mean asking, "So if I can get you a better price, you'll take it?"
- Clarifying does not mean asking, "What will it take to get your business?"
- Clarifying does not mean asking, "Is that the only thing holding you back?"

This last one boxes the customer into a corner and is regarded as a high-pressure sales tactic. Although this type of approach does work, it puts customers on the defensive. This is also considered to be a "tie down" question, designed to get the customer to make a commitment. It may work but it certainly doesn't build trust. In fact, it just reinforces the concept that salespeople are concerned *only* with closing the sale.

If you really want to stand out from your competition, learn how to use this process when customers present objections. Resist the temptation to begin offering a variety of solutions immediately.

Let's apply the concepts of empathizing and clarifying to the objections most retail salespeople face.

"I'll think about it." "Sure. I can understand that. A lot of my customers like to think about their purchase. What is it that you'd like to think about?"

"I need to check with my spouse." "I can appreciate that. I'm married too and I check with my spouse when considering a major purchase. What concerns do you think he/she might have?"

"It's too expensive." "I can understand your concern; it is a major purchase. Do you mind if I ask why you feel that way?"

"I'm going to look around." "Sure. I think it's wise to look around before you make a final commitment. What is it that you hope to find?"

"I'm still shopping around." "I can appreciate that. I usually shop around too. What is it that you hope to find?"

"XYZ company has it for a lower price." "They do offer some competitive prices there. Is it that you don't see the added value of buying from our store?"

"It costs more than I planned to spend." "I can appreciate that. You came in with a certain budget in mind and now we're exceeding it. So you like this product; it's just more than you planned to invest, is that it?"

"I'll be back." "Great! I'm glad to hear that. Tell me, is there a particular reason you're not interested in making your decision today?"

"I don't get paid until Friday." "No problem, I can appreciate your situation. So you like this product and you'd just like to wait until you get paid on Friday, is that right?"

"No, I don't think so." "No problem. I respect your decision. Is there a particular reason you don't want it?"

Exercise

You may not feel comfortable with all of these responses—and I don't expect you to. Before reading further, take a few minutes and read each of the above responses aloud at least three to five times. This will help you become more comfortable with this entire process.

Did it feel repetitive? Redundant? Unnatural? Good! You're perfectly normal. There are two reasons you should feel this way:

1. The words on the previous page are not yours and you aren't likely to feel comfortable using them. As you move through this book you will have the opportunity to create your own responses to the most common objections you hear from your customers.

2. This is a new skill and the key to learning any new skill is to practise it over and over and over again.

If you completed the previous exercise you are ready to move on. If you chose not to do the activity . . . STOP! Go back and read aloud each of the responses on the previous two pages. It will help you with the next exercise.

Personalized Responses

Exercise

Copy the objections and my suggested responses from the end of the previous section onto another sheet of paper—or use the worksheet provided in the action planner at www.stopasklisten.com—leaving several lines of space for your own responses to each. At this point, you should have a better understanding of how the empathizing and clarifying process works. Now put on your thinking cap and create your own responses in your words. Here are a few guidelines to consider as you work through this exercise:

1. I have provided my responses to each objection. If you are comfortable with those, make no changes. There's no point trying to recreate the wheel.

2. If you want to tweak the response just a bit and change only a few words, do so.

3. If you would prefer to change the entire answer, then do that.

One word of caution: don't begin moving toward overcoming the specific objections. Avoid statements such as, "Were you aware that . . . ?" or "Did you know . . . ?" or "Can I tell you . . . ?" Now you are ready to create your responses.

How did you find that exercise? If you found it challenging, you're not the first to feel that way. Many other salespeople would agree with you.

This component of the professional sales process tends to be the most difficult for most people to fully understand, accept, and learn to execute. The reason is simple. Most salespeople automatically react by trying to solve objections directly. They think that the process outlined here will take too long and that they can more easily provide a direct solution to the objection. To this I would point out that if you know exactly what you are trying to overcome, you will actually save time. Rather than spin your wheels offering a solution to what you *think* the objection might be, uncover the real objection first. Then you can apply a solution that is really appropriate to that customer's needs and situation. For example, if the customer's concern revolves around budget and you concentrate on adding value, you are probably not going to close the sale.

Exercise

Take a few minutes and practise the responses you just developed further. State each response aloud three to five times. This exercise may seem redundant and repetitive at this stage. That is exactly its purpose! *I cannot urge you strongly enough to resist the temptation to skip this exercise.* Make the time to complete it. Carrying it out will help your brain and mouth work together so that when you hear one of these objections in the course of your regular workday, you will know how to respond and what to say automatically.

Stop and review your responses aloud now.

There are several do's and don'ts you need to keep in mind when empathizing and clarifying your customer's objections.

- Do listen to the customer. Don't assume you know what he is going to say.

- Do ensure your tone of voice conveys true empathy. Don't just rattle off the words; you'll come across as phony and insincere.

- Do be patient. Uncovering a customer's true objection will take a few moments. Don't be in a rush to get to the root of her hesitation.

- Do pause before you respond. Don't rush your answer. Customers will respect you if you carefully plan your response rather than appearing as if you have a scripted answer for everything.

Step 3—Seek Permission

This means that you ask your customers for their permission to offer a solution to their objections. You do this to make them more receptive to your solution. Your seeking permission puts the customer in a better state of mind. If you just barrel ahead and offer a solution after you've empathized and clarified, the customer will still be slightly on the defensive so your solution may fall on deaf ears.

Once you have verified the customer's objection and she responds positively, simply ask if you can provide a solution: you are asking permission to overcome her objection.

Customer: "I'll think about it."

You: "No problem. I usually think about my purchases too. Is there something specific you wanted to think about?"

Customer: "Well, it's more than I planned to spend."

You: "I can appreciate that. You came in with a certain budget in mind and we've exceeded it, is that right?"

Customer: "Yeah."

You: "Would it be okay if I took a moment to explain some of the options available to you?"

In this situation the salesperson listened with empathy and continued to clarify until she uncovered the customer's true objection. Then she bridged by asking permission to provide a solution.

The value in taking this approach is that the customer will be much more receptive to your feedback: first, because you have asked for permission and second, because she gave you that permission. When someone gives you permission to solve the objection, she is more likely to listen to your solution than start wondering how she is going to get out of the store. Notice, too, that the sales process will shift to more of a dialogue than an attempt to push the customer into making a decision.

In rare cases customers will not grant you this permission. If this happens, you have two options:

1. You can thank them and then walk them out the door. "Thank you very much for dropping by the store. If there's anything I can do for you please let me know." If they don't want you to overcome their objection there is not much you can do. Most of the time, this doesn't happen if you've applied the other steps in the sales process properly.

2. The second alternative is to repeat the empathizing and clarifying process with this objection. "No problem, not everyone is interested. Do you mind if I ask why?" Some salespeople cringe when I suggest this because they feel that the customer will think they sound too pushy. I believe that you have nothing to lose at this point. There must be a reason why the customer does not want you to provide a solution. In many cases you will find that he just does not have the time to hear it at that particular moment. That

being so, your response should be, "I can appreciate that. When would it be convenient to discuss these options?"

If you use the appropriate tone of voice you won't sound pushy or aggressive. If you have established a high level of trust and a strong rapport with your customer, he will permit you to ask such questions. What you've done earlier in the sales process always affects what happens later in the same process.

As I mentioned earlier, most salespeople move immediately to solving the objection rather than empathizing, clarifying, and seeking permission. Here are more advantages and benefits to following these steps outlined here:

• You will reduce the customers' potential hostility.
• You will earn more trust from them.
• You will thoroughly understand their objections.
• You will make them more receptive to a solution.
• You will give yourself some additional time to formulate a response.

Once you have reached this stage, you can offer a solution. I provide no scripted responses to each objection because I feel that you need to adapt your response to meet each customer's specific needs. I repeat here: If you have done your job effectively in the earlier stages of the sales process, you should know what is important to him or her by this time.

Step 4—Provide a Solution

The final step in handling objections is to provide a solution to the customer's objection. I cannot repeat too often that I don't believe in scripted answers for objections—except for empathizing and clarifying—as every customer is different and requires a different response.

The real key to solving objections is to fully qualify your customer. I have learned from personal experience, the importance of investing the time upfront finding out as much about the prospect as possible. In one sales discussion, everything seemed to be moving along nicely. I had several conversations with my contact and submitted a proposal. Unfortunately, I failed to ask one simple question—"Who else is involved in this decision?" As it turned out, my contact had two other business partners whom I knew absolutely nothing about. They hadn't been involved in any of the discussions so when they reviewed the proposal, they concentrated strictly on the price of the service I had planned to provide. In the following pages are some additional tips and strategies that will further help you.

Overcoming the Price Objection

Regardless of what you are selling and to whom, you face price objections. Allow me to present a different perspective of this obstacle. If you have established a high level of trust and a strong rapport and have focused your presentation around the customer's needs, price will be a less important issue. Price will continue to concern the customer; it will less likely be the primary issue.

Case in point: In the situation I described in Chapter Four— shopping for the washer and dryer valued at $1300—I did not like or trust the salesperson who latched onto my wife and me. Consequently, I worked him hard on price, asking for many concessions. I liked the store and knew the level of post-sale service was good, but I wanted to make the salesman work hard, *very hard*, in order to get the sale.

In another situation—buying the broadloom for our house for $2100—the salesman built more of a rapport with us. During the entire sales process he demonstrated interest in us, he asked us questions and he made us feel comfortable. Although I negotiated for a better price I didn't grind him hard.

When we bought a new fridge and stove—for $1800—the sales associate established even more rapport and trust than the one selling the broadloom had. I asked for a price reduction, but I admit I didn't push very hard for a discount.

Was price a factor in these purchases? Definitely. The difference between each was the level of trust and rapport each salesperson developed with us. People are less likely to be difficult with someone they like and/or trust.

Another way to overcome the price objection is to add value as you progress through the sales process. This doesn't mean you drone on and on and on about the merits of your service and knowledge. It means you act differently from the way your competition does. Ask careful open-ended questions, listen attentively to the answers, and allow your customer to do most of the talking. The simple techniques will prove to your customer that you take her seriously and are concerned about her—not yourself. Stating this makes it sounds simple; salespeople seldom do so in the real world. They are so intent on closing the sale that they feel they must push hard. In fact, if you take the opposite approach and focus on your customer, he will close sale for you—and with much less resistance!

I once had the good fortune to work with a man who epitomized this concept. He very rarely concentrated on closing, regardless of the pressure he might have faced that particular month. He asked his customers good questions, paid attention to the responses, and adapted his presentation to meet their specific needs. When in each case the time came to discuss price, he had already demonstrated that he was worth the sticker price on whatever product he was selling and he seldom discounted—although many of his co-workers did.

KISS Your Customer

Assuming you have been able to progress to this point with the customer and he has granted you permission to overcome his objection, keep one additional point in mind. KISS your customer!

Keep It Short and Sweet.

When salespeople attempt to overcome objections they tend to talk far too much. In many cases they don't recognize when they have provided an adequate answer to the objection. Other times, they sound as if they are trying to justify why the customer should buy from them. In short, they come across to the customer as desperate.

Your goal is to talk for no more than 20 to 30 seconds before you check with the customer to see if the solution you suggested is appropriate. For example, "Mr. Customer, we offer a full, unconditional 30-day return policy if the product does not meet your expectations. How does that sound to you?" If he says no, seek permission again: "Could I give you another reason to buy from us?" When he grants you that permission, provide just one more solution, saying, "We also . . . How does that sound?" You will quickly find this approach much more effective than rattling off a long list of reasons why the customer should decide to buy from you.

There is another reason why you should avoid presenting several options or solutions to a customer. If the customer objects yet again, you will find you have run out of ammunition. Assuming you lived somewhere with snow in winter, think back to organizing snowball fights when you were a child. If you were smart you would somehow let your opponent know when you ran out of snowballs. This bolstered his confidence and he would then attack you with a little less caution. Then, as he got close enough, you dived behind your fort, reached for your backup supply, and BAM!—caught him off guard. Even as children we knew instinctively that we should not throw away all our firepower too quickly.

The same holds true when overcoming customers' objections. If you give away all your ammunition at once, you'll have nothing to fight with. (The term "fight" has been used as a metaphor only. I am not suggesting that you view the process of overcoming objections as a fight or battle. This must be done in a professional, non-threatening manner.)

The real key to overcoming objections is to invest the appropriate amount of time qualifying your customer earlier on. Effective qualifying will reveal your customer's motives for wishing to make the purchase in the first place. Also, you will learn what the customer's hot buttons are—information you can use to your advantage in the entire sales process.

Summary

1. Distinguish between a condition of sale and an objection: A condition of sale is something that is out of your control. An objection is something you can provide a solution to.

2. Empathize—Express in your own words your understanding of the customer's point of view. "I understand how you feel. Other people have felt the same way."

3. Clarify—Restate the objection back to the customer in your own words to ensure that he fully understands his objection. "So what you're saying is that you don't see the value in this, is that right?"

4. Seek permission—Ask the customer for permission to solve her objection. "Would it be okay if I took a moment to explain some of the benefits of purchasing from us?"

5. Solve the objection—Offer a solution that is appropriate to your customer's specific needs and situation.

6. Practise your empathizing and clarifying scripts—Learn how to respond to every objection you hear.

7. Deal with the price objection by showing that you are different from your competition. Focus on building rapport and fully understanding the customers' needs.

8. When offering a solution, KISS your customer. Keep It Short & Sweet.

9. Invest the appropriate amount of time qualifying your customers, and you will have fewer objections to deal with.

Action Plan

In your action planner, answer these questions:

1. What did you learn about overcoming objections?
2. How will you apply this information?
3. What will you do differently on your next shift?

Telling the Customer to Buy

"Earn the right to ask your customers for their money."

If you have:

- greeted your customers with something other than "Hi, how are you today?"
- asked them sound, open-ended questions to uncover both their logical and emotional needs,
- listened carefully to their responses,
- given a dynamic presentation of your product or service that focuses on meeting their specific needs,
- painted mental pictures by using descriptive words and telling stories,
- handled their objections by listening with empathy, clarifying those objections, and then asked permission to offer solutions,
- presented solutions that are pertinent to their specific situations,

then you've earned the right to ask your customers for their money.

Buying Signals

Before you ask for a sale you'll have to recognize some of the buying signals customers give us. In your action planner, list a dozen or so clues that customers give you to let you know they are interested in making the purchase.

Did your list include the following?

- The customer comes into the store with an advertisement, either from you or your competitor.
- He goes directly to the item he wishes to buy.
- Her eyes light up when you present and discuss the product.
- He involuntarily reaches for the product.
- A couple asks for time to discuss it.
- She asks questions about warranty, stock availability, delivery, colour/style options.
- He shows excitement.
- She becomes more animated.
- He begins to agree with you.
- She talks about the product using words denoting ownership.
- He makes positive statements about the product.
- They ask about payment or financing options.
- She says, "I'll take it."

Although this last point seems quite obvious to read here, many salespeople miss it completely. They are so intent on talking about the product they miss the customer's most obvious buying signal. I was once approached by a salesperson to purchase a game for one of my training sessions. The game's concept interested me, and after reviewing the materials and listening to the sales presentation, I told the salesperson that I would like to take it. He replied with, "If you want some time to think about it, it's no problem. You can call me when you've made a decision."

Apparently, he was paying no attention to me or he was used to hearing "no" as a response. I actually had to tell him that I wanted to buy it two more times! I have often wondered how many sales he lost because he didn't pay attention to his customer.

Does this mean that if a customer sends out one of these signals you should ask for the sale? Not necessarily. Your goal is to watch for a combination of buying signals. One or two clues indicate some readiness to buy—several signals demonstrate a stronger desire.

Customer Fears

Closing is a natural part of the sales process, providing you have done everything else right. And even if you have executed the concepts we have discussed here, you still need to be aware of one more thing. Many customers experience certain fears or hesitations that may prevent them from making a buying decision.

What fears or hesitations do you think they experience? Write down some of these fears in your action planner, and then compare your list with the one below:

- Fear of paying too much. It is not unusual for a customer to purchase an item only to find the identical item on sale a few weeks later, either at your store or from one of your competitors.

- Fear of obsolescence. Advances in computers and electronics technology, in particular, have fuelled this fear in many consumers today.

- Buying the wrong product. Will it really do what the salesperson says it will?

- Not being able to use a complex product—again, particularly true of electronics and computers. (This fear can overlap with the second point above.)

- What other will people say about the purchase. Many of us have bought something and then had a relative or friend comment to us that we made a poor decision or paid too much.

- Simply making a purchasing decision. Consider how often people will agonize over a relatively insignificant purchase. We salespeople stand there, impatiently waiting for the customer to make a decision, thinking to ourselves, "What's the big deal? The tie only costs $35."
- Being taken advantage of.
- Lack of trust in you as the salesperson. Customers may not be sure you will follow through on your commitments and/or promises.
- Fear of your stores or company going out of business. Given today's economic challenges, many consumers are understandably concerned about your company's ability to stay solvent and competitive.

It is absolutely critical to recognize that most customers will hesitate just before they make their final decision. Often some unspoken issue arises for them at this moment of truth. Sometimes they will express these concerns in the form of comments or objections. More often, though, they will keep their last-minute concerns to themselves. This means that you must be in tune with your customers to help encourage them to share their concerns. If you have taken some care with effectively qualifying the customer's needs and building a good rapport with him, you've gone a long way toward reducing this final hesitation. When you have established an excellent relationship with your customer, he is less likely to feel these fears and hesitations. Obviously, the size of the purchase also plays a part in this uncertainty as well. If she is buying a $79 purse, she will hesitate less than she would if she were purchasing a $3000 living-room set.

Even if you're not able to overcome these fears or hesitations at this stage, you can let your customer know that you empathize with them. Remember, your goal is to make your customers feel good about their purchase and to give them a reason to buy from you.

Personal Fears

Retail sales staff often grapple with their own fears at this point of the sales process, too. Our most common concerns are listed below. Place a check mark beside the concerns that most affect you:

- rejection
- losing the sale
- coming across as being pushy or rude
- lack of confidence
- realizing the item is out of stock
- doubting the product's quality
- awareness that you can't afford to buy the product
- assumption that the customer can't afford it
- never having sold an item of that magnitude before
- not knowing how to ask for the sale

There are several ways to deal with each of these issues.

First, recognize that would-be buyers know it is your job to ask for the sale. And, in many situations, they *want* you to ask. A workshop participant once told me of an encounter he had with a businessman to whom he was selling a television. This sales associate had invested the time qualifying the prospect and showed him a TV that met the customer's expressed needs. Approximately half an hour elapsed and the customer was just standing silently in front of the television with his hands thrust deeply into his pockets. A barrage of questions and concerns raced through the sales associate's mind as he tried to figure out what to do next. Finally, he blurted out, "Is there anything else I can do?" The customer looked at him intently for a few moments, then replied, "You can ask me if I want it." After the sales associate picked himself up off the floor, he asked for, and closed, the sale.

Remember, if you've done everything we have talked about throughout the process outlined here, then you have earned the right to ask the customer for the sale.

The other way of dealing with your own hesitations is to ensure that you have followed the sales process. Check that you have gathered as much information as you can, learned exactly what the customer needs and wants, and, most importantly, be confident. If you have done everything you should have done, you should be sure of yourself in asking for the sale. People want to buy from confident salespeople.

Here are 10 additional points about overcoming your own personal fears:

1. Rejection—This is by far the biggest killer of sales. Since most people want to be liked and accepted by others, this concern looms large in our minds. As salespeople, we take "no" personally; we equate it with a personal attack. Unless we have done something grossly wrong, the customer is rejecting the product, not us. The world of retail sales is a numbers game, regardless of what we sell and whom we sell it to. Recognize that rejection is part of the game no matter how well we do our jobs.

2. Losing the sale—This runs a close second to the preceding fear, particularly for commissioned salespeople. Once we have invested time, effort, and energy with a customer, we tend to agonize over what will happen if the customer does not finally buy. We view our investment as lost time and money. True sales professionals accept this as a natural part of the sales process. We know that not every sale will be consummated. There will always be someone else to sell to.

3. Coming across as pushy or rude—This concern, too, ties in with the fear of rejection. We don't want to offend other people and we think that asking for the sale will do exactly this. Here are two considerations. If we have a) established a high level of trust and a strong rapport during the sales cycle, and b) kept our tone of voice and body language positive, we will

not appear pushy. Remember, people expect you to ask for the sale.

4. Lack of confidence—Many times, we feel this fear because we lack knowledge of our product; we remember negative sales situations in the past; or we are relatively new to this particular sales environment. Try these approaches:

    i) Learn as much about your product as possible. The more you know about what you are selling, the better you will be able to help customers determine which models or items will best suit their needs. You will be able to answer questions confidently, regardless of what people are asking.

    ii) Decide to let go of any baggage you are carrying around from previous sales situations. What is done is done. To be truly successful in sales you need to learn to concentrate on the present or future, not the past. You cannot change the situations that have already taken place; you can influence how you respond today.

    iii) If you are new to sales or your position, or store, learn as much about the company as you can. Talk to your co-workers, observe other sales transactions, read any information the company makes available, and attend training sessions. Many retailers offer sales training or product knowledge online; take advantage of these opportunities to increase your knowledge and skill.

    These three strategies can help bolster your confidence for the moment when you are poised to ask for the sale.

5. The item may not be in stock—Many salespeople assume that the customer will be unwilling to wait for the product if it is currently out of stock or on back order. We can deal with this before it arises by qualifying the customer's needs properly. What other store has she visited? What has she seen? When does she need or want the item? Does the competitor have it in stock? Inventory has always been and always will

be a contentious issue in retail. A fact of retail life is that no store in the world has every product in stock when a customer needs it. Of course, some retailers manage their inventory more effectively than others do. Recognize that most customers will wait, providing you give them a reason to and that the purchase is not an impulsive one. Ensure that your customers appreciate that you differ from your competitors, give them a reason to buy from you, and many times they will wait.

6. Your own lack of belief in the product's quality—This fear arises in many retail stores, and for a variety of reasons.

   • You question the price at which you sell it compared to your cost to buy it.

   • You know your competitors sell the identical item for much less.

   • You know the item has a history of returns or repairs.

   Our priority must be straightforward: if the customer is interested in the product, it fits his needs, and he likes it, he will see the value! It doesn't matter what we think; we are not the buyer!

7. Awareness that you can't afford it—Although this is not an issue in all retail stores, it can be a major barrier to your closing the sale in plenty of them. I worked for an electronics retailer where a television can cost more than $6,000! I can't afford that! Plenty of people can afford such prices, though, so it does not matter what salespeople can or cannot buy ourselves. Such a fear should never limit your ability to ask for the sale.

8. Assumption that the customer can't afford it—This is one of the greatest mistakes you can make, and salespeople all make it. You base the fear on the way a customer is dressed, his mannerisms, or his speech. I have seen grubby, dishevelled customers pay cash for a $2,000 item. This is your customer's decision—not ours.

9. Never having sold an item of that magnitude—if you have been used to selling T-shirts and now you're selling high-end furniture, the transition can be difficult and will take some time. Recognize that everything is relative and you will soon become accustomed to selling higher-ticket items.

10. Not knowing how to ask for the sale—This is the easiest to overcome. Learn and practise asking. Years ago I was selling a seminar to the restaurant industry. I went out on my first call and delivered my presentation. My prospective customer began sending me strong buying signals. She even told me outright, "That looks good; I like it."

    I was caught off guard and was not sure what to do next since I had not had any formal training in sales at this point in my career. I was waiting for her to say, "I'll take it," and, unfortunately, she did not use those words. I mustered up all my courage and asked, "So, when would you like to arrange the training?" We set a date and I closed my first sale. Had I not asked, I am sure the sale would not have happened. There are many non-threatening ways to ask for the sale. Here are 14 examples:

    - Is that the one you'd like to go with?
    - How will you be paying for that?
    - Would you like to put this on your _____ card?
    - Would you like me to check on the availability?
    - When would you like it delivered?
    - Let me get one from the back for you.
    - Which of these do you prefer?
    - Let me check to see if we have it in stock.
    - We have a few in stock—would you like one?
    - Can I write this up for you?
    - Shall I get started on the paperwork?
    - Is this the one for you?
    - Can I wrap this up for you?

- Based on everything we've talked about, I think this one best suits your needs. What do you think?

Exercise

These are just a few general closing questions you can ask. In your personal action planner, record your own additional questions that are relevant to your particular retail business.

Regardless of whatever hesitations you feel, remember that it is your job to ask the customer for his money. "You can read all the books on selling, watch all the sales videos, listen to all the success tapes. If you don't learn to ask for the sale, you're going to go broke."

I can't count the number of times I have been willing to make a purchase and the salesperson has failed to ask me for the sale. In those situations when I have been somewhat indecisive and no one has encouraged me to make the purchase, I have chosen to pick up the item later. Inevitably, the laws of the universe then take over, work against me, and

- the item wasn't in stock when I returned;
- I became too busy and didn't make the time to return; or
- I forgot to go back.

Each of these is a lose-lose situation for both of us that could have been prevented if the salesperson had followed through on the entire sales process. The salesperson only had to encourage me to take that final step.

How to Close More Sales

Once you have asked a closing question,
BE QUIET.
Many a sale has been lost because the salesperson just could not keep his or her mouth shut after asking for the sale. Once you ask for the sale, remain silent!

One of the most common mistakes made by salespeople is not allowing the customer the opportunity to make that decision. When the customer does not respond immediately, the salesperson jumps in and begins to talk again.

Keep in mind what is happening when you ask the customer for the sale. She is processing information. She is running through her options, justifying or rationalizing her purchase, and mentally ticking off the features and benefits that she has on her list. For example, you ask, "Would you like to go with that one?" The customer starts thinking, "Let's see. It has all the features I wanted. The salesperson seems pretty knowledgeable, so if I have any questions after I get home, I think he'll be able to answer them. It fits my budget. I like the look of it. I think that's everything."

This entire mental dialogue takes mere seconds. Unfortunately, when the customer does not respond immediately, we begin our own mental dialogue that goes something like this. "Oh no, she hasn't answered yet. She looks as if she's upset about something. I bet she saw it at dealer XYZ at a lower price and I *know* she's going to grind me on that. Either that or she's just going to walk out and buy it there. Then what will I do? I just spent all this time with her showing her why it makes sense to buy from me, and now she's probably going to get it somewhere else. Or maybe I missed something? Maybe I forget to tell her something. Yeah, that's it."

Then we blurt out something stupid like, "Have you seen it cheaper somewhere else?"

We have now accomplished two unfortunate things. We have interrupted the customer's train of thought. *And,* we have introduced him to a fresh potential objection. Now, I don't know about you, but I think selling is challenging enough without handing our customers' objections. Being quiet until they respond on their own will help you avoid this.

I am often asked by participants in my workshops how long they should wait before they speak. I always say wait for the customer to respond before you say another word, regardless of how long that takes. You have asked a question . . . wait for the response. In our culture, we are not used to silence. We are uncomfortable with it. I used to have this problem myself when I first started training. I would finish a particular segment and ask, "Are there any questions?" I'd scan the room quickly, and if no one asked a question within three or four seconds, I'd move briskly on to the next topic. What I have learned is that it often takes as long as 20 to 30 seconds before participants can formulate questions. They are busy thinking about what was discussed, how it applies to their situation or workplaces, how they can use it, and perhaps rationalizing the information. It takes time for them to process it and produce a response to my question. I now wait patiently until someone responds.

Think of spreadsheet software as an analogy. If you create a complicated spreadsheet in Excel or Lotus, your computer requires a certain amount of time to process the information and calculate an answer. If you press the ESC button during this processing time, you interrupt the computer and prevent it from completing the task. Interrupting a customer by blurting out a statement or asking a question has exactly the same effect. Show respect for your customers: wait for a response.

Here are two techniques to feel more comfortable with this silence.

First, recite your license plate number backwards. This removes your attention from the immediate situation and gives your brain something to do. Be careful not to mentally check out completely, though. If you do, the customer will notice it in your eyes and you will lose all the credibility that you have worked so hard to gain.

The second method is to run through everything you and your customer have talked about in your own mind. Review how you have built a bond with him and visualize him acting positively to your question. Both of these methods will help distract you from the silence. Handling these awkward few moments is not all that difficult to learn. All it takes is practice.

Closing Techniques

There are a variety of closing techniques and strategies you can use. Here are a few of them.

The Summary Close. You summarize what you have discussed during your presentation. "Okay, Mr. Smith, let me see if I can recap where we are. If you get this . . . , you will be able to [summarize]. Is that a fair summary of how you see it too?" This close is particularly useful if you have invested a significant amount of time with your customer or if he has been into the store several times.

The Choice Close. Here you ask the customer to choose between two alternatives. You can phrase this close as a question or a statement. "So, Ms. Johnson, which of these two do you prefer?" or "You seem to be deciding between these two models."

The Suggestion Close. As the term implies, you suggest the decision with this close. "So based on what we've discussed, this looks like the one that's best for you. Should I get started on the paperwork?" Remember that many customers need approval before making a decision to buy. This type of close is ideal for this type of customer.

The Direct Close. If the customer's comments are signaling very high interest, a simple direct response or question can often finalize the sale. "Will that be cash or on a credit card?" or "I can arrange to have it delivered first thing tomorrow morning." When you use a direct close, your language—both verbal and non-verbal—must be positive and your attitude confident, not pushy. This increases your chances of getting a positive response to this closing strategy. Nothing you say or do should convey uncertainty, doubt, or hesitation.

The Testimonial Close. It can help to alleviate the customer's fear of making a mistake. Draw on your own experience and reassure her that she is making a smart decision, by providing a testimonial from a previous customer or by telling a favourable story about the product. Use any written testimonials you have available. People are more likely to believe what they see in writing than what they hear.

The Assumptive Close. This is one of the simplest and most effective closing techniques because it does not place any emotional stress on the customer. This close makes the assumption that the customer is going to buy. "When you get home, take the time to read through the manual," or, "Your son will be so happy when he opens this up." This type of close often paints a mental image in the customer's mind and can influence her decision by transferring ownership to her. She begins to see herself using the product in the environment for which she's considering buying it.

The Justification Close. Here, summarize all the product's benefits in point form. The total impact of all the list will often give the customer the justification he needs to go ahead with the purchase. It also reminds him of any selling points that he may have forgotten from your presentation. This technique can be very useful when the customer is trying to convince himself that he should make the purchase. With larger, more complex purchases, this close demonstrates the value the customer will enjoy in making the purchase.

The Puppy Dog Close. Many years ago, on a Friday night, a mom and dad in a pet shop were deciding whether or not to buy that adorable pup. The owner or salesperson said, "Why not take him home for the weekend? If you decide you don't like having a dog around, bring him back on Monday, no questions asked." How many people would actually bring back a furry little puppy dog after several days?

This close persuades the customer to buy the product, bring it home, and use it for several days. The law of psychology almost guarantees that in nearly all cases the customer will not return the product once she has had it in her possession for that time. "Take it home with you. If you don't like it, you can return it within 30 days." However, I advise you to use this type of close only as a last resort, when the customer really is not sure whether she is going to be completely happy with the product.

The Tag-Team Close. This technique works best when the customer still cannot decide whether to purchase the item. A co-worker or manager steps in and comments warmly about the product. "That colour looks great on you," "This item is very popular. You're going to love it." This reinforces the customer's earlier interest and can ease his fears about making the wrong decision.

The customer perceives that the third party has no personal stake in closing the sale. That person will earn no commission. She will not benefit from the sale. Also, people want reassurance.

They want to know that they are making the right decision.

I hope you noticed that none of these strategies or techniques is manipulative or pushy. They all strive for the same result and they should not offend your customer in any way.

Ultimately, the most effective way to close a sale is to follow through on the entire sales process. Implement what we have discussed so far. Instead of focusing on closing the sale, concentrate on the sales process. Too many sales people try to force the sale. This is comparable to *pushing* a piece of string—which is virtually impossible. Although you can pressure people into a buying decision, your goal is to develop long-term customers by using a consultative approach. The real key is to show your prospective customer why she should buy from you rather than your competitor. This means you ask her good questions, demonstrate enthusiasm, show interest in her needs, present your products in a lively manner, handle her objections properly, and employ a variety of closing techniques.

In the real world, of course, the majority of salespeople *do not* give their prospect a compelling reason to buy. Sure, they have talked extensively about the product or service; they have discussed all the features and benefits; they have tackled every objection. Yet this does not mean they have earned the right to ask for the customer's money.

Closing *should* be a natural extension of everything else you have done. You cannot force the sale to happen. Actually, I take that back—you *can* force it. But you will seldom generate repeat business or loyal customers this way.

If, on the other hand, you follow the concepts discussed here, you will gain the trust of your would-be customer; you will demonstrate that you differ favourably from your competitors; customers will consider price a less contentious issue; and they will sell themselves on your product or service. You won't need to force sales! Concentrate on understanding your customers thoroughly, ask sound questions, allow them to do most of the talking—and they will close the deals themselves, happily.

You are ultimately responsible for making that sale happen, no matter how well customers participate with you in the process. You must ask them to make that decision. You must ask for their money. It is not their job to say, "I'll take it"; it is your responsibility to have uncovered their needs, to have shown them how the product meets those needs, to have established the value of your product or service, and then to have asked them for the sale!

Summary

1. People exhibit a variety of different buying signals. Pay attention to your customers and watch for the clues that may indicate their interest in making a final decision.

2. Understand that virtually every customer will have some fears or hesitations at the moment of truth. If you have developed an excellent relationship with her, she will be less likely to hesitate.

3. Overcome your personal fears about asking for the sale by fulfilling your obligation as a sales professional and following the concepts in this book. Acknowledge that it is your responsibility to ask for the sale.

4. Learn to ask a variety of closing questions.

5. Be quiet after you ask a closing question.

6. Familiarize yourself with using different closing techniques.

Action Plan

In your action planner, answer these questions:

1. What did you learn in this chapter?

2. How will you apply this information?

3. What are you prepared to do differently on your next shift?

4. What difficulties do you anticipate?

5. How will you deal with these challenges?

Selling to the Opposite Sex

"Men are from Mars, Women are from Venus."
—John Gray

In the late 1990s I worked for a prominent consumer electronics chain. After conducting a series of focus groups, we discovered that we were missing potential sales opportunities with our female clientele. Further research uncovered that women and men have different sets of criteria when they shop for a product. In recent years, several books discussing this issue have also surfaced and the results are consistent—the shopping behaviours of men and women differ significantly.

This chapter is dedicated to helping you learn the differences between men and women in the buying process. If you are a female sales associate, you will discover what changes you need to make to improve your sales results with male customers. Male sales staff will learn the most common mistakes they make when dealing with women in their stores.

Let's start by comparing how men and women view the shopping process.

Two Different Perspectives

Research indicates that men see shopping as a necessity while women view it as an experience. Watch how women behave in a grocery store compared to men. Unlike men, who run in and out of a store, women will often peruse the entire store. Men will pick out the items they need, toss them in a cart, look at their list, and head directly to the next aisle. On the other hand, women will walk up and down each aisle, read labels, compare brands, and explore options.

After more than 20 years of marriage, I have learned that it is a rare situation when my wife runs out for something and returns quickly. In the past she has stated, "I'm just going to the mall to pick up a few things. Do you want to come with me?" I have learned the hard way that such a venture could actually take several hours. As a man, this is not the way I prefer to spend my time. Christmas shopping is another example. My wife will spend several days locating the perfect gift for each person on her list. When I am tasked with the shopping, I take the list, head to the mall and when I stumble across an item that meets the criteria for that particular gift, I buy it. I do not comparison shop. I do not visit three or four stores to see what they have to offer.

There is nothing wrong with the way either gender approaches the shopping process—we are just different. We also make decisions differently.

Making a Decision

Men tend to move through the decision-making process quickly. A man will ask himself a few basic questions:

- **Does this item meet my needs?**
- **Will it solve my problem?**
- **Is it what I am looking for—features, price, etc.?**

Assuming these questions are answered, he will make the purchase. Men also tend to be more impulsive buyers than women. Many men will make significant purchases very quickly or with seemingly little consideration. This does not mean, however, that men do not think about their purchase.

Women will ponder their options, talk to other people, usually women, and do more research than the average man. Women will consider the purchase from many different angles, will make more comparisons, and will use more sources of information. For example, my wife will call her sister and talk about an intended purchase. When the conversation is finished, she will call another friend and seek her opinion as well. She will search the Internet for information, compare it with the facts she has in her possession, return to the store, and ask a few more questions before finally making a decision.

If you try to push a woman customer to make a decision too quickly it will backfire on you and you will likely lose the sale and any potential future business from her.

Buying Needs

As noted in Chapter Four, all customers have certain buying needs—either logical or emotional. Asking the right questions will help you determine each customer's requirements.

Men tend to focus on their logical needs when making a purchase.

- **Does the product have this feature?**
- **Can it do this particular thing?**
- **Is it the weight I need?**
- **Does it have the power I'm looking for?**
- **If I buy it, will it be able to do what I need?**

Generally speaking, men are not comfortable asking questions until they become comfortable with the salesperson; that is why we seldom ask for directions! This discomfort increases when they are shopping for a product they are unfamiliar with.

However, you can quickly make them feel at ease if you use the right approach. I recently visited a pet store with the intention of adding several fish to my aquarium. The salesperson approached me and asked if I needed help. Because I wasn't sure what fish were compatible with my existing fish and was hesitant to ask, I declined his assistance. A few moments later he asked, "What do you currently have?" This prompted me to tell him, after which he was able to point out what would be suitable for me.

Spend less time talking and building rapport. Instead, concentrate on helping him find exactly what he is looking for. If you do decide to make small talk stay focused on topics that men are most comfortable talking about—sports, money, and business. And when you talk about your product or service, demonstrate how it will address his specific logical needs.

Women usually have more emotional needs when they make a buying decision. They will focus on how the item fits into their lifestyle, how it will make them feel, and how the purchase will affect other important people in their lives. Ask plenty of open-ended questions to make women feel more comfortable in the sales process. Encourage her to open up and share information by asking questions such as:

- **"Tell me about your previous unit . . . "**
- **"How was your experience at . . . ?"**
- **"What did you find that . . . ?"**
- **"What would you like to see changed this time?"**

Questions such as these are effective in learning exactly what she wants and needs.

Women will likely give you more background information about their purchase than men. A man will say, "I need a new fax machine," while a female customer is more prone to say, "I've been getting a lot busier lately. My last fax machine worked okay for the first two years; then it kept jamming every time I received a fax. I've tried to fix it, but I'm not really good with these things. I've been getting aggravated because I don't have time to reset the paper every time I get a fax." Although for male sales associates, this seems like more information than is necessary, it actually demonstrates that she is beginning to trust you. Plus, in her mind, everything she told you was relevant to the purchase.

What Did You Say?

Communication is another area in which men and women differ. Men tend to be very direct, often blunt, in their communication. Women are much more subtle and indirect in their conversations. If a couple is driving along the highway and the wife sees a restaurant approaching, she will often ask, "Are you hungry?" This is an indirect way of saying, "Honey, I'm hungry. Can we stop at the restaurant?" Unfortunately, the husband is unaware of the hidden message and responds with a no. She asks, "Are you sure?" The husband displays some irritation and says, "I'm sure." The car passes the exit for the restaurant and the wife is fuming because she thinks her husband didn't listen to her. I have been married for over 20 years and have just clued into this in the last few years!

When I ask my wife what time she would like dinner, I often hear, "I have a few phone calls to make. Then I have to pick up our daughter at the train station and drop her off at dance class. And then I need to stop at the store for a few items." What she is doing is working through her schedule to figure out how long it will take her to do all those errands. Then, she will tell me what time she wants dinner. When men are asked this question, they usually respond directly with, "Six o'clock."

Both genders will also make the same statement about a product but it will have two completely different meanings. Here is an example: "I'm glad this car has ABS brakes."

Both enjoy the fact that they will able to stop more quickly; but the woman is thinking how safe her children will be in the car, while the man is thinking how fast he will be able to drive.

Another difference in our communication styles is the way we listen. Women are very attentive listeners. They make constant eye contact and nod frequently to show they are paying attention. Men will listen, but they may not necessarily look at you while doing so. When I traveled a lot I would return from a business trip on Friday evening, and as I flipped through the mail, my wife told me about her week. Although I was listening to her, my lack of direct attention and eye contact gave her the impression I wasn't paying attention. I soon learned that I needed to look at her to demonstrate that I was paying attention.

Generally speaking, women require more eye contact to feel that they are being listened to. When you talk to a female customer, look her directly in the eye for at least three to four seconds before looking away. Male sales associates may feel uncomfortable with this because they think that prolonged eye contact is a sign of flirting. I can assure you, your female clientele will not think you are flirting with them! However, you will establish yourself as a great listener and this will quickly gain their trust.

Men Selling to Women

If you are a male sales associate and frequently interact with female customers, this section will help you learn what changes you need to make in various steps of the sales process to become more effective.

First, focus on establishing a relationship with her. Look her directly in the eye as you shake hands. Do this immediately to establish a business relationship and to show respect. Soften your initial contact by asking, "Is there something particular you're looking for?"

Instead of jumping to a discussion of your product or service, invest the time learning about her specific needs. Ask more questions than you would a male customer. Give her plenty of opportunity to express what is on her mind. As mentioned in Chapter Five, most salespeople have the habit of telling customers too much. Avoid this mistake with all customers, but be particularly aware of it with your female clientele. Condition yourself to listen more and talk less.

Remember to ask primarily open-ended questions. Soften your probing questions by starting with, "Would you mind if I asked you a few questions?" This is less direct and will make her feel more comfortable responding to you. Whenever possible, avoid using questions that begin with "why." These types of questions will cause her to feel that you are challenging her and make her become defensive. When my oldest daughter decided to spend a summer working at a resort, she told me she was going to bring seven pairs of shoes with her. I asked her why and she immediately became defensive. When I rephrased the question to, "What made you decide to bring seven pairs of shoes with you?" she opened up and told me her intent.

Paraphrase what your female customer tells you so you fully understand her needs. Restate her needs back to her in the form of a statement as opposed to a question. "You want a model that will automatically shut off," instead of "So you want a model that will shut off automatically?" The latter question can sound condescending to women. The advantage to using this approach is that it will encourage her to share more information with you.

Start the sales presentation by stating, "Based on what you told me..." This will prevent your customer from thinking that you are giving her advice. It is reminding her that she expressed several needs and you are now about to show her how your product or service will help her.

Avoid using jargon, acronyms, SKUs, model numbers, or terminology that she may be unfamiliar with. This applies to all customers, but it is even more relevant to women. Do not make her feel intimidated or you will lose the sale faster than you can blink.

Most women are always thinking of other people so incorporate people into your presentation. "You will love driving your son to baseball practice in this SUV. It will make you feel safe and secure." "Your parents will be thrilled to have e-mailed photos of your daughter." Use feelings, words, and emotions to describe the product and her use of it. This may be difficult for you in the beginning and it will feel unnatural. However, I guarantee that your customers will respond favourably.

Take your time moving through the sales process. Keep your ego in check—this is not a competition. Avoid playing "oneupmanship" with women. They simply don't play this game and it will appear that you are boasting.

Avoid asking, "What will it take to get you to buy today?" or "What do I have to do to get you into that this afternoon?" You will offend most women with a direct question like this. Ask softer questions such as, "How would you like to proceed?" or "What would you like to do next?" or "Tell me what you think." This is a gentler way of asking a woman to make a decision.

Women Selling to Men

This section will show female sales associates the changes to make in your approach when dealing with male customers.

Be confident. Start the conversation by asking, "Tell me, what are you looking for today?" This may feel very confrontational, but most men appreciate the direct approach and will not be offended.

Pay attention to what is important to men—money, sports, business. Familiarize yourself with the headlines in the business section of the newspaper, sports terminology, and current standings. You can have most of this information emailed to you everyday from various websites on the Internet. You do not have to become an expert but you do need to be knowledgeable.

Men are not comfortable with all products. In these situations, ease into the conversation by asking a closed-ended question such as, "Do you have...?" This will help him become more comfortable and relaxed.

Recognize that most men will usually state their needs clearly and directly. However, they do not usually provide as much detail as you, a woman, would give. As long as the information they provide is enough for you to make an educated decision about the best product or service for their specifics, disregard asking more questions. However, if you require additional details use more closed-ended questions.

To develop credibility, state your credentials early in the sales process. "I have worked in this industry for over seven years and worked with many men in your situation." This will position you as an expert and make him more comfortable with you. Your product knowledge will also contribute to this. Think back to my example in Chapter Four when I was looking for a new garment bag and the sales clerk did not know which products were durable. The more complicated your industry (or male-dominated it is), the more important product knowledge becomes. Invest the time learning everything about your products.

Use humour to break any tension and to establish credibility. Be careful not to use self-deprecating humour because it will actually reduce your credibility from a man's perspective.

Focus on the logical elements of the item. Again, product knowledge is important because it will help you show yourself as an expert. Avoid becoming emotional during the sales process. The more emotional you become, the more likely your male customer will become rational.

If you do not have the answer to a question, admit it. But do not apologize profusely. You need to be direct and say, "I don't know. I will find out." This is much more effective than "I'm not sure. I could probably ask someone, but I'm not sure who the best person would be. Um, maybe we could look for the answer in this manual." Get to the point quickly. Men want to get to the bottom line fast. If you take too long to get there, they will tune you out.

Do not be afraid to ask for the sale. Men expect you to ask and a direct approach will not surprise or offend them. Practise asking questions such as; "Would you like to go ahead with this?" or "Why don't I get started on the paperwork?" or "Which of these do you prefer?" You may find these questions very uncomfortable at first. I guarantee that you will notice a difference in your sales—immediately!

Lastly, here is a final note about behaviour. Avoid making assumptions! Just because a woman is hesitant-sounding or apologetic, it does not mean she will be easy to close. You must invest the time establishing trust, uncovering her needs, and demonstrating why she should buy from you. And, although initially daunting, a direct and blunt male customer may buy immediately if given the right reasons.

Summary

1. Men and women view the buying process differently. Men see shopping as a necessity, but women see it as an experience.

2. Women generally take more time to make a buying decision. Avoid trying to push her into making a quick decision.

3. Men tend to respond better to closed-ended questions, particularly at the beginning of the sales process. Women prefer to answer open-ended questions.

4. The buying needs of women tend to be emotion-based. Men's needs are usually more product-focused or logical. Adapt your approach accordingly.

5. Men tend to be very direct in their communication. Female sales associates should not be offended or concerned by this directness.

6. Women communicate with more subtlety. Male sales associates must learn to be patient, read between the lines, and ask clarifying questions.

7. When selling to men, get to the point quickly. Focus on developing a business relationship with your female customers.

Action Plan

In your action planner, answer the following questions:

1. What new information did you learn from this chapter?

2. What changes do you have to make to improve your overall effectiveness?

3. What challenges do you anticipate?

4. What will you do to address these challenges?

chapter nine

Maximizing Your Sales Opportunities

"If you saw a $20 bill lying on the sidewalk, would you leave it there?"

At this point in the process, many salespeople think their job is done. They have closed the sale. Whew! Breathe a sigh of relief and move on to the next customer. But wait! You have probably left some money lying on the counter. While you may not have left cash there literally, you haven't maximized your sales opportunities and revenue potential.

This chapter will explore how to sell add-on items and accessories without being pushy. We will take a look at selling intangible items such as extended warranties, maintenance programs, and fabric protection. We will also discuss the importance of referrals and how you can ask for them.

Accessorizing

In most retail stores, accessorizing represents a missed opportunity to greatly increase our chances of earning an excellent income. Far too often, we are so focused on the primary sale, or getting to the next customer, that we neglect further opportunities to increase our sales and our profitability. No sales are complete unless the customers have been given every chance to accessorize their purchases. Whatever we sell, we can always suggest add-ons. Perhaps the organization that best succeeds in this is McDonald's. Regardless of what you order, the counter person asks you if you'd like something else—dessert, a salad, a soda. And these are teenagers! If these minimum-wage order-takers can learn how to accessorize—suggestively sell—it should be a piece of cake for you.

Consider these examples:

If you sell...	Suggest...
Eyewear	*Protective cases, cleaner*
Electronics	*Batteries, power bars, high-quality patch cords and cables, extra batteries for remote controls, extended warranties, cleaning products, bags, lenses for cameras*
Pets	*Food, treats, toys, cleaning supplies, deodorizers, shampoos*
Furniture	*Fabric protection, extended warranties, lamps, pictures, coffee and end tables, other accents*
Clothes	*Ties, socks, belts, jewelry, scarves, shoes, cuff links, tie clips*
Shoes	*Shoe trees, polish, cleaner, arch supports, insoles, conditioner, fabric protection*
Jewelry	*Cleaner, jewelry box, other jewelry*
Refrigerators	*Cleaner, extra ice cube trays, extended warranties*
Stoves	*Cleaner, extended warranties, baking sheets, pots and pans*
Washer/Dryers	*Fabric softener, detergent, extended warranties, cleaner*

Sports equipment	*Laces, leather conditioner, cleaner*
Office supplies	*Paper, pens, staples, highlighters, file folders, Post-It notes*
Party supplies	*Cards, ribbon, favours, additional decorations*
Patio Furniture	*Accents, umbrellas, plants, wall hangings, candles, candle holders, mosquito and pest repellents*
Computers	*Disks, paper, ink cartridges, software, power bars, storage containers for disks, CD-ROMs*
CDs	*Jewel cases, CD cleaner, carrying cases*
Home Furnishings	*Place mats, fruit bowls, candle holders, napkins, napkin holders*
Swimming Pools	*Chairs, toys, chemicals, flotation devices*

There is virtually no limit to the accessorizing possibilities. All it takes is a bit of initiative and creativity.

Many salespeople make the mistake of assuming that their customer will ask for specific accessories. This is not always the case. When my wife and I bought our first computer, we could hardly wait to get home, set it up, and become a high-tech family. I unpacked the boxes and began plugging in everything. Unfortunately, I ran out of receptacles before I completed the setup. I didn't have an extra power bar handy so that meant I had to get back in my car, drive to a store, wait in line to buy one, and return home before I could enjoy my new toy. A good power bar in a computer store can cost over $100, yet I choose to go the closest store where I picked an inexpensive one for around $12. Would I have paid more at the computer store? Willingly, providing the salesperson had done his job properly.

Another concern about accessorizing is that some salespeople feel they will come across as being pushy if they keep suggesting more accessories. In fact, the customer will tell you when she reaches her limit. Several years ago, I was in the process of buying two new suits. The two salespeople who assisted me—the store was pretty quiet that day—kept suggesting ties, shirts, socks, and belts. I accepted some suggestions, rejected others, until I felt I had enough variety and selection. The result was an additional $400 in revenue for the store. My original budget was shot to heck, but at no time did I feel pressured or coerced into making my purchases. I had the right and ability to say no at any time. If the salespeople had not suggested the accessories, I might have bought one or two ties, but certainly not the three or four I ended up with along with the shirts and several pairs of socks. Eventually, when I left the store, I felt great because I knew that I had several options every time I planned to wear one of those suits.

Accessorizing is part of the sales process and must be treated as such. Don't wait until the end of the sale to begin mentioning add-on items. Incorporate them into your sales presentation. This will mentally prepare your customers for the additional expense and make it easier to sell to them.

Exercise

To help you get started, take a few moments and jot down some of the accessories you can suggest with specific products and the best time to discuss them with your customers. Record your responses in your action planner or on a separate piece of paper.

Product	Accessory	Best Time to Discuss

Selling Intangibles

Many retailers sell intangible items (extended warranties, fabric protection, service plans, maintenance programs). Unfortunately, negative publicity in the media and aggressive, unscrupulous sales tactics have made it more difficult to sell these less-tangible products.

There are three separate strategies that, when combined, will improve your overall results. These techniques are the introduction, discussion, and asking for the sale. As I present these ideas, I will use the term "extended warranty" to describe the intangible item.

Strategy One—The Introduction

The introduction sets the stage for the remainder of the process. To achieve the best results, you should introduce the extended warranty early in the sales interaction, ideally during the qualifying process. Tell the customer that the item qualifies for the additional coverage. This begins to prepare the customer for the additional expense and also creates the opportunity for you to discuss the extended warranty later in the sale. Here is how it works.

Once you learn what product the customer is interested in buying, you start by stating, "You'll be happy to know that this camera comes with a one-year warranty. It also qualifies for our extended service plan, which I'll tell you more about later." Pause briefly before continuing to ask questions to explore the customer's needs. Notice the use of the word "qualifies." Qualify is a subtle yet powerful word. It intimates that not all products have the option of the extended warranty—which in most retailers is accurate. People enjoy being able to qualify for something. Vendors at trade shows and conferences use this approach and ask you to submit your business card to qualify for a free draw or prize. What makes this approach most effective is the use of the pause. You plant the seed of being able to qualify for the extended warranty, pause briefly to allow that information to sink in, and continue to uncover the customer's specific needs and wants.

If you sell extended warranties, you have several opportunities to introduce them: the standard introduction, the replacement product, and the direct approach.

• *Standard Introduction*

The introduction I used on the previous page is a standard one and is best used for the typical sales interaction. I recommend stating it as soon as you learn what type of product the customer is looking at. "All of our vehicles come with a three-year, 60,000 kilometre warranty. Plus, they all qualify for our Peace of Mind program, which I'll tell you about later. What type of vehicle were you most interested in?"

• *Replacement Product*

When customers tell you that they are replacing an existing item because it broke down within the first few years, you can use this approach. This tends to happen with portable items or high-use products.

First, empathize with them. "That's too bad. It must be frustrating to have to replace it so soon." Pause. Then say, "You'll be happy to know that all our cameras qualify for a five-year warranty." (This makes the assumption that you offer this type of coverage.)

This approach is extremely effective; the customer has already experienced a relatively short life cycle with one product, and you have just explained that you can extend the use of the new one.

• *Direct Approach*

This is the most difficult introduction to use, but it can be one of the most effective. This particular approach requires you to ask your customers if they have ever purchased a warranty of any type in the past. "Mr. Customer, just for curiosity's sake, have you ever purchased a warranty on any of the products you own?" The value in asking a direct question like this is that you quickly uncover the customer's perspective on extended warranties.

Some customers will respond with a vehement "No!" Others will say no, they don't believe in them. Some people will tell you about their previous experiences, usually negative, and a few customers will say yes. Although this can be a challenging approach for many sales associates, it quickly tells you how your customer views extended warranties. That means you can plan your approach accordingly. For example, if someone says, "I never buy warranties," you can respond with, "Not everyone does. Do you mind if I ask what your reasons are?" They will likely tell you the reasons behind their decision, which, in turn, gives you the necessary information to properly position your particular program.

An early introduction of the extended warranty, maintenance program, fabric protection, or similar program is one of the keys to consistent success. Train yourself to look for the opportunities to plant the seed of the additional coverage and mention it early.

One word of caution—at this stage, your goal is to simply introduce the program. Do not discuss the features, benefits, coverage, or cost. Remember, you have not yet fully uncovered the customer's needs and wants. If your customers ask for more information when you introduce the extended warranty, resist the temptation to give it to them. Instead, say, "I'll be more than happy to tell you about it once we find the product that best suits your needs." Then ask a well-thought-out qualifying question. In only a few situations will your customers pursue the issue. If they do, tell them about one feature and benefit of the program and then return to the qualifying process.

Strategy Two—Discussing the Program

The second strategy for maximizing your sales of an intangible item is discussing it properly. The most common mistakes made by salespeople when they discuss their extended warranty are these:

1. They lack complete knowledge of the program.

2. They wait too long to begin talking about it.

3. They spend too much time discussing it.

4. They lack confidence presenting it.

Mistake #1—They lack complete knowledge of the program.

As discussed in Chapter Five, product knowledge is crucial. Yet too many salespeople do not know as much about their extended warranty as they should. They know one or two key features but are not aware of all the details of the program. Make the time to familiarize yourself with the program(s) your company offers. Familiarize yourself with the features, read the fine print, and review the contract. You must also know the corresponding benefit for each feature.

Exercise

In your action planner, record the features and benefits of your specific program. For example,

Feature: It allows you to extend your warranty coverage for up to five years.

Benefit: Worry-free enjoyment of your product for up to five years.

Feature: It covers 100 percent parts and labour.

Benefit: You will not have to pay any out-of-pocket expenses.

Mistake #2—They wait too long to discuss it.

Too many salespeople wait until the end of the sales process before mentioning their extended warranty program. "Oh, by the way, we have an extended warranty program that you might be interested in." This approach is not very effective because the customers have already started to mentally check out. They are no longer in the buying mode. During this transition they calculate their purchase, including the appropriate taxes; decide on their method of payment; and begin thinking about their next task. This process takes just a few seconds and they begin to tune you out, closing the door on their mental bank.

Mistake #3—They spend too much time talking about it.

Ineffective salespeople create a separate presentation for their extended warranty program. In fact, they often spend more time talking about this program than they do the product. The majority of salespeople tend to tell their customer about every feature their program has to offer. Unfortunately, this shotgun approach lacks impact, because it seldom addresses the customer's specific needs. The majority of customers lose interest, and this means they will not hear some of the information you present.

The most effective way to discuss the extended warranty is to integrate it into your entire product presentation. As you point out certain features and benefits of the product, discuss an aspect of the extended warranty that relates to that particular feature. Mention just one feature of the extended warranty and return to your product presentation. Repeat this process several times. Here is an example:

- "Mr. Customer, based on what you have told me, this particular voice recorder will be best for your needs. As I mentioned earlier, it also has a one-year warranty that can be extended to a full five years through our Customer Maintenance Program. This unit comes with an eight-megabyte memory card, which means you will be able to record up to an hour of information. You can also purchase additional cards to give you more recording time."

- "As you can see, this unit is very compact. Sometimes the cards can get jammed, particularly if you inadvertently try to insert them upside down. However, if you choose to add the Customer Maintenance Program to your purchase, we will take care of removing the card for you at no charge."

- "This is the power adapter, which allows you to plug it in rather than using batteries. And here are the headphones that will allow you to listen to your recording with privacy. The Customer Maintenance Program I mentioned will cover any repairs to the jacks if they are required."

Notice how the discussion of the Customer Maintenance Program was integrated into the overall explanation of the product. This approach makes the extended warranty seem more like an actual feature of the product rather than a separate purchase.

Generally, after you mention it two or three times, the customer will ask a question like, "What does it cover?" or "How does the program work?" or "How much does it cost?" These questions are great because they usually mean that the customer is interested in the extended warranty. When this happens, answer their questions directly and with confidence.

Mistake #4—They lack confidence presenting it.

Lack of confidence often stems from not possessing a real belief in your specific program. You may feel that the price is too high in comparison to the price of the product. You could be the type of individual who does not personally believe in extended warranties. You might have encountered opinionated customers in the past. Regardless of the reason, this lack of confidence will come across loud and clear to your customer through your words, tone of voice, and body language.

Your choice of words must demonstrate confidence. Avoid using weak words such as "You might," "I think," "possibly," and "perhaps." Replace them with, "You will," or "I know." Eliminate "possibly" and "perhaps" from your vocabulary as you tell someone about your program.

Your tone must be positive and confident. An unsure, hesitant voice will send the message that you expect resistance from the customer. Record your presentation so you can hear exactly how you come across to your customer. Make notes on how you can improve your tone to project confidence.

Your body language will make the strongest impact on your customer. I once saw a sales associate actually tug at his collar as he told his customer the price of the extra coverage. This definitely showed the customer that he, the sales associate, was not comfortable talking about the price of his product. People believe what they see more than what they hear. It is critical that you maintain positive body positioning and make great eye contact while talking about your extended warranty.

Strategy Three—Asking for the Sale

Many people do buy extended warranties. Yet many sales associates fail to ask for the sale. My wife seldom buys anything without an extra warranty and is always surprised when the salesperson does not ask for the sale after she has given strong buying signals, like "What kind of warranty does this come with?" followed by "Can I get more than that?"

If you have followed the process outlined in this chapter, asking for the sale is a natural step. The key is to avoid making any kind of assumption. The most common assumptions salespeople make are these:

• The customer can't afford it.

• The customer won't see the value.

• This particular customer won't buy extra warranties.

• This item won't need the extra coverage.

• The purchase is too small and the price of the extended warranty is too high.

Unfortunately, these assumptions penalize everyone involved—the sales associate, the company, and the customer. Do yourself a favour and ask *all* your customers if they want the extra coverage your company offers. Here is a different perspective on why this is important:

When I bought my Palm Pilot, I did my homework and shopped at a few stores. When I made my final decision, I also planned to buy the extended warranty the store offered. I was extremely busy at the time I made the purchase and was thinking about an upcoming appointment rather than the sales process. Fortunately the sales associate asked me if I wanted the additional coverage, because I completely forgot to mention it.

Avoid making the assumption that the customer will not be interested. Ask her for the sale.

Three Steps to Guaranteed Success

Here are three steps that will guarantee sales success of your intangible items.

- Step One—Introduce early in the sales process.
- Step Two—Discuss frequently in your sales presentation.
- Step Three—Ask for the sale.

The key here is to follow these three steps with *every single* customer you talk to—assuming, of course, that the product qualifies for the intangible item. If you avoid making assumptions and mention it to every customer, every day, you will consistently reach your quota. This sounds easy in theory; in actual practice it is much more challenging. However, the top salespeople in retail chains who sell intangible items make it a point to inform every customer about their particular program. They also ask for the sale—every time!

Referrals

Another way to increase your sales immediately is to ask for referrals. If you are serious about building your business, you must become serious about asking for these. In the retail environment, I have seldom encountered salespeople who use this approach consistently. The most common excuses they give me:

- "I'm not comfortable doing that."
- "My customers will think I'm being pushy."
- "If I do my job properly, my customer will automatically recommend me."

To explore each of these in more detail:

1. *"I'm not comfortable doing that."* The primary reason we may feel uncomfortable is that we remember situations when a salesman has approached us for a referral and the experience has left a bitter taste in our mouth. This means we will hesitate to ask a customer for additional business ourselves.

2. *"My customers will think I'm being pushy."* If you have done everything effectively during the entire sales process and you then ask for a referral in a non-threatening, non-aggressive manner, your customer will not view you as pushy. In fact, in most cases, he will be happy to recommend a friend because he will want to share his positive experience with others. When people buy something, especially a major purchase, they are usually in a highly charged emotional state and want to share that experience with others. Asking for a referral will help you help them achieve that goal.

3. *"If I do my job properly, my customer will recommend me automatically."* This is accurate in part. However, this perception lacks one small detail. Let's assume I have just bought a new TV from you. I invite some friends over to watch a movie and one of them comments on the television. My response is something like, "I got it at ABC Electronics. They were really helpful there. In fact, I'd recommend them to anyone looking for a TV." Although I did recommend the store, I didn't mention your name, which means my friends won't ask for you specifically. That is why it's critical to tell your customers to recommend you.

Here's a simple, effective method to ask for referrals that doesn't sound pushy or rude. *"If you've been happy with the service I've provided and know someone who could benefit, have them give me a call."* Then hand them a business card. This gentle method of asking for business differs greatly from some of the experiences I have had myself, such as financial planners or insurance reps thrusting a blank sheet of paper at me and demanding the names of 10 relatives or friends. I don't consider this latter approach a professional way to generate business. Although it may work, I doubt it creates a positive lasting image in the customer's mind.

Assuming you have handled the referral aspect of selling properly, how do you deal with the referrals once they start to show up in your store?

Obviously, you are going to take care of the new prospect as well as, if not better than, you did your original customer. It is also important to handle the person who referred the new client to you properly. Here is what to do:

- At the very least, call the customer who referred the new customer to you, regardless of whether the new prospect actually purchased anything. Thank him for thinking of you and let him know you appreciate his doing so.

- For a stronger impact, send a thank-you card to your original customer. You can write something like, "Dear Mrs. Smith, thank you for sending Pat Jones in to see me. I appreciate your thinking of me and I look forward to doing business with you again soon." Sign it and enclose a business card. This simple gesture is incredibly powerful, in part because so few people make the effort to thank their customers in writing. We are besieged with phone calls every day and we often forget the callers by the end of the day. However, when we receive a handwritten card from someone we take notice. Usually, we end up saving it. In fact, I still have thank-you cards that I received years ago.

- If your original customer continues to send in more prospects, consider rewarding her. You don't have to buy a lavish gift; often a small token will be sufficient. Send something that is relevant to his interests and hobbies. For example, if this customer enjoys cigars, buy a good-quality cigar from a quality tobacconist or, perhaps, the latest issue of *Cigar Aficionado*. A simple gesture like this will encourage your customer to continue recommending others to you.

- If you handle this element of your business effectively, you will quickly develop an excellent reputation and plenty of new and repeat business. Certainly, this aspect takes effort, energy, time, and discipline to carry out. Wouldn't you rather put the effort into this instead of cold-calling prospects in order to reach your sales targets? In short, work smarter, not harder.

What Impact Can Referrals Make?

Referrals can make a huge difference in your overall sales during the year. Consider the impact of being able to generate just one referral each week. This works out to 50 new clients each year, assuming you take two weeks' vacation. If the average sale in your store is $200, this could mean $10,000 in extra sales. If you were to generate one referral a day, this would increase to $50,000 a year. How much commission do you earn on $50,000? Obviously, it will depend on your company. Some pay their salespeople on a sliding scale. Others pay a flat rate. Or you may work for an organization that pays its sales staff a straight hourly wage or weekly salary.

My point is that you can earn more money without working additional hours or shifts and without working harder. Your closing ratio will be much higher with these referrals, since you will enjoy a certain level of trust with your new prospects. You'll now find yourself dealing with warm leads as opposed to cold ones. Customers will be more likely to accept your feedback, suggestions, and ideas because one of their friends has recommended you.

Word-of-mouth advertising is the best means of advertising. Recommendations by other people influence our purchasing decisions. Consider these examples:

- When you need a real estate agent, financial planner, or lawyer, do you not ask your friends for a recommendation?
- How often do you ask friends to recommend a restaurant?
- If someone asks you for feedback on where to buy or fix a car, don't you answer based on your personal experiences?

- Caterers, hairstylists, consultants, trainers, professional speakers, architects, contractors, and tradespeople such as electricians, plumbers, and woodworkers all rely on referrals to stay in business.

There is nothing inappropriate about asking for a referral to generate more business. In fact, the more referrals you ask for, the more business you will get.

The Sale Follow-up

If you really want to stand out from your competition and give people a reason to buy from you, keep in touch after you have finalized the sales transaction with them. Depending on where you work and the way your store processes sales, this may not always be possible, but, if you work in an environment that records customer names for each purchase, you have a tremendous opportunity to increase your sales this way.

First, recognize that most salespeople at most retailers promptly forget about the customers once they walk out the door. If you make a concerted effort to contact those customers after they have purchased something from you, you will strengthen the relationship developed during the sales process.

Consider this example. After my wife and I bought our first house, we never heard from our real estate agent again. Yet the agent who represented the sellers has been in touch with us countless times. She has sent us newsletters, calendars, and Christmas cards. She even sent us a card to celebrate our first anniversary in our new home. She also sends a fridge magnet once or twice a year. Who do you think we will think of when it comes time to sell this house and buy a new one?

When you make the effort to follow up after the sale, it sends your customers the message that you see them as more than one-time sales. You show them that you value their business. You demonstrate why they should continue to buy from you. You can carry out this follow-up in several ways:

1. You can call customers on the telephone and ask how they are enjoying their purchase. The call could go something like this: "Hi, Mr. Smith. This is Kelley calling from the Running House. I'm just calling to see how you are enjoying the running shoes you bought last week." Don't try to sell them something; simply enquire about the products they recently purchased. You will be surprised at the impact this gesture will have on your customers.

2. Send customers a card thanking them for their business. It does not have to be expensive or embossed. A simple card with a handwritten message is a powerful tool.

3. Keep in touch with them. Let them know of promotions, upcoming sales, or additional products they might enjoy. You can do this by telephone, mail, or email. Find out what type of communication your customers prefer.

4. Invite them to special events you organize. Events such as preferred-customer days or sneak previews will often draw people back to your store. A good friend of mine has a customer appreciation night once a year. He organizes some form of entertainment and supplies plenty of food and drinks. This gives his customers the opportunity to network with one another.

Your goal is to encourage your clients to return to your store and become loyal shoppers. Don't expect immediate results. Developing a loyal customer base takes hard work and continued effort over a lengthy time, even years.

These concepts will help you increase your sales. All you need to do is implement them.

Summary

1. Accessorize every sale. Learn which accessories most suit each product and suggest them to your customers.

2. Continue suggesting accessories until the customer tells you to stop.

3. Introduce your extended warranty or similar program early in the sales process.

4. Discuss your extended warranty program frequently during your sales presentation by mentioning just one feature and benefit at a time. Integrate your discussion of this intangible item into your overall product presentation.

5. Ask every customer if she would like to buy your extended warranty program.

6. Learn how to ask for referrals. Recognize that these can generate additional revenue without your having to work harder.

7. Ask every customer for a referral. "If you've been happy with the service I've provided and know someone who could benefit, have them give me a call."

8. Send cards to customers who refer other people to you. Give them a reason to send you other referrals.

9. Organize special events for your customers. Show your customers that they are appreciated and valued.

Action Plan

In your action planner, answer these questions:

1. What did you learn about maximizing the sale?

2. What will you do differently on your next shift?

3. What challenges do you anticipate?

4. How will you deal with these challenges?

Harnessing the Power of Goals to Achieve Sales Success

"A goal is simply a dream with a deadline."

Goal setting is an integral part of our lives whether we realize it or not. Many people state that they don't set goals because they don't want to set themselves up for failure. It is vital to understand that, as human beings, we have a deep-seated need to set goals for ourselves. We need targets to focus on to keep us motivated.

One of the greatest motivators for people is to have worthwhile and meaningful goals to strive toward. These include business goals as well as personal aspirations and targets. Challenging goals encourage us to accomplish more, to achieve more, and, if properly planned, to enjoy life more.

In this chapter you will learn the importance of setting goals in both your business and personal lives. You will understand why people do not set goals or achieve the goals they do create. You will learn the SMART process for setting goals and how to create action plans that will help you achieve your targets.

Why Set Goals?

Goals give you focus, clarity, and direction. Powerful goals will motivate and excite you. Goals can help you enjoy a fulfilling and rewarding life. Goals will cause you to grow. They will help you learn. Most importantly, they help ordinary people achieve extraordinary things.

According to business author Brian Tracy, Yale University conducted a study in 1953. They interviewed all of the graduating students, determining who had established clear goals and plans. The results indicated that only 3 percent of the students had set clear goals. Twenty years later, the researchers interviewed the same students again and discovered that the 3 percent who had clear goals were worth more in financial terms than the remaining 97 percent combined.

This research clearly demonstrates the importance of setting goals.

What Is Stopping You?

There are a variety of reasons why people do not set goals.

- They don't know how to set goals.
- They are afraid of failing.
- They are afraid of succeeding.
- They think it is too difficult and will take too much time.
- They do not want to move from their existing comfort zone.
- They don't believe that the process works.
- They are afraid to make a commitment.
- They don't want to take the time.

Let's examine each of these for a moment.

They don't know how to set goals. This is one of the most common reasons. Regardless of your education, it is highly unlikely that you were given any instruction on how to set goals for yourself. Few institutions provide courses on setting goals. Yet learning the appropriate way to set and achieve goals is a powerful life strategy.

They are afraid of failing. This response is a close runner-up to the previous reason. The majority of people have a high resistance to failure, which is a normal human reaction. However, failure is a part of life. We all fail. Consider these facts:

- Stephen King was not able to pay for heat when the manuscript for his first novel was accepted.
- Walt Disney went bankrupt several times before he built Disneyland.
- Henry Ford failed and went broke five times before he succeeded.
- Babe Ruth struck out 1,330 times. He also hit 714 home runs.
- Abraham Lincoln went bankrupt and failed in business twice and lost eight elections before he became President of the United States.
- Thomas Edison failed over 10,000 times before he developed the light bulb. He also experimented over 17,000 times before he developed the plant from which latex is derived.
- Colonel Sanders was rejected over 1,000 times before he sold his secret recipe for chicken.
- Dr. Seuss was rejected by 23 publishers before he found a publisher who would print his first book. It sold 6 million copies.

Each of these individuals experienced serious setbacks before achieving greatness.

They are afraid of succeeding. Surprisingly, this is a very common fear. We become fraught with concerns. What happens if I sell too much? My boss will want me to do it again. My budget will be increased. What if I can't repeat my results? Will I have to work harder? Or longer?

This was one of my greatest concerns when I chose to leave the corporate world and start my own business. I value my personal time and initially thought about the consequences if my business grew too large, too quickly. I have since determined that I will not allow this concern to limit or restrict me from developing my business. I have made the conscious decision that I *want* to be successful and will manage the business to ensure it does not intrude on my personal life.

They think it is too difficult and will take too much time. Setting goals and creating action can be relatively easy once you develop the discipline to do so. It takes practice, particularly at first. Once you get into a routine, you will find that establishing goals does not take much time.

They do not want to move from their existing comfort zone. Humans love routine. And goals force us out of our comfortable routines. This is why change is so difficult for most people to deal with. We get accustomed to following a particular routine in our day. When we are forced to make a change, it disrupts this natural flow. I used to experience this when I worked in the hospitality industry. When we made a menu or operational change, it always took a few days for everyone to incorporate the new procedure into their day. Eventually, though, people adapted and the change soon became the new routine.

They don't believe that the process works. This is not an uncommon belief. I remember talking to a salesperson who said, "I don't set goals. That way I don't feel disappointed when they don't happen." One of the reasons people lack the belief in goals is that they have set them in the past but were unable to achieve them. This is usually due to an unrealistic expectation, like, "I want to lose 30 pounds this month."

They are afraid to make a commitment. Many people think that once they commit to a goal they will not be able to change their mind, focus, or direction. Although this is not the case, it is important to recognize that this commitment is often needed in order to achieve the goal. The more challenging the goal, the higher the level of commitment required.

They don't take or make the time. Let's face it—we are all busier now than ever before. As a result, we often do not make the time to clearly establish what we want to accomplish. However, this planning helps clarify our path and will give us the focus we need to achieve better results. A few hours each month can go a long way in helping you accomplish more than you thought possible.

Why People Fail to Achieve Their Goals

Many individuals set goals on a regular basis but have difficulty achieving them. Here are the top 10 contributing factors:

1. They do not write down their goals.
2. They do not create action plans.
3. They do not take action.
4. Their goals are not motivating enough.
5. They set unrealistic time frames to achieve their goals.
6. They try to accomplish too many goals at the same time.
7. Their goals are determined by other people.
8. They give up at the first sign of difficulty.
9. They forget about their goals.
10. They try to accomplish everything on their own.

These reasons are all valid and affect most people, so it is worthwhile to discuss each of them.

They do not write down their goals.
Many people set goals for themselves but keep them in their head. Although they have taken the first step, it is not enough to simply keep your goals in your thoughts. To truly activate and harness the power of goals, you need to record them on paper. Actor Jim Carrey was once interviewed and he talked about a cheque he wrote to himself when he was young. It was for starring in a movie, and it was made out for several million dollars. He kept this cheque in his wallet and looked at it frequently. Many years later, he was paid $10 million for a movie.

Write out your goals every day. This helps plant them deep into the subconscious and reinforces your desire to achieve them. Ideally, write your goals first thing in the morning and again just before you retire for the night. I make it a habit to record mine every morning before I start work. For some people this may seem like a lot of work and not worth the effort. I have recently begun using this approach and can report incredible results. It takes just a few minutes to jot your goals down in a notebook and the rewards can be astounding.

They do not create action plans.
Goals without action plans are not complete. They are similar to a pilot flying an aircraft without a flight plan. Action plans identify the specific steps you need to take to achieve your goals. Action plans provide the focus and direction to help you move toward their accomplishment. We will discuss how to create action plans later in the chapter.

They do not take action.
Action generates results. Thinking, writing, and planning are important. But you cannot expect to become the top salesperson in your store if all you do is plan your strategy. Taking one or two steps toward the completion of your goals every day will propel you forward faster than you dreamed possible.

Their goals are not motivating enough.
Weak or unmotivating goals do not generate a powerful internal desire. Goals must be challenging, inspiring, and motivating.

You must get excited about achieving the targets you have set for yourself. An excellent way to generate this motivation is to create a list of benefits for each of your goals. When I chose to quit smoking I identified 75 reasons why this goal was important to me and how I would benefit. I carried this list in my DayTimer and reviewed it regularly. When I experienced cravings this list helped me stay on track. Your goals *must* be meaningful to you.

Their goals are determined by other people.
This is a common situation in sales. The sales manager decides the quota for each salesperson without the individual's input or feedback. The goal is actually the sales manager's, not the employee's. The result is a half-hearted attempt by the salesperson to achieve this target.

The people who are responsible for achieving the goals should be involved in the process. This causes concern for many sales managers because they believe the quotas their team establishes will not meet the company's expectations. The most effective way to manage this is to discuss the company goals with your team. Explain the rationale behind the corporate goal and enlist their support. Discuss the importance of reaching those targets and ask your team for their assistance. A company I once worked with took this approach after many years of telling everyone what their targets needed to be. When everyone had finished working on their individual goals the outcome was higher than the corporate expectations. Enlisting your team's support and assistance and involving people in the goal-setting process increases buy-in, which leads to better results.

They set unrealistic time frames to achieve their goals.
There is no such thing as an unrealistic goal—just an unrealistic time frame for accomplishing that goal. Virtually any goals can be attained if we are given sufficient time to work on them. It is possible to lose 25 pounds in five months, but to lose that weight in two months would be very difficult, not to mention unhealthy.

The larger or more challenging your goal, the more time you need to allot to achieving it. I will, however, add a qualifier to this statement—if you allow yourself too much time to attain your goal, it will become less challenging and motivating.

They try to accomplish too many goals at the same time.
Some people work on dozens of goals simultaneously. This diffuses their efforts, which means they will not have the focus necessary to achieve their most important goals. Opinions vary as to the ideal number of goals you set for yourself. I believe you should be working on 10 to 12 goals at any given time. These should be broken down into four categories: short-term (less than one year), mid-term (one to three or five years), long-term (five years or longer), and life goals, which may take as many as 20 years to accomplish. Many of your short- and mid-term targets will be smaller versions of your long-term and life goals. Here is an example of the goals I typically have for myself at any given time:

- Three to four monthly targets
- Two or three goals to achieve in a three- to six-month time frame
- Three annual goals
- One or two goals to accomplish in five to seven years
- One goal I want to achieve in the next 15 years

When I reach my short-term targets, I automatically move closer to achieving my long-term and life goals.

They give up at the first sign of difficulty.
This is one the most valuable lessons I have learned about achieving goals. It is inevitable that you will face obstacles as you progress toward your goals. Some of these obstacles will seem virtually impossible to overcome. This is what causes many people to give up. Yet managing those obstacles, and finding ways to get past them, will help you achieve your goals. This is what separates the most successful people from everyone else.

Anyone can set a lofty target. Only the truly determined will persevere until they succeed. A close friend of mine was once engaged in a bitter lawsuit. After many months of legal battles he thought of a strategy that eventually helped him win. When I asked him how he thought of that particular strategy, his response was, "It was the only thing left to do."

In many cases, it is that last obstacle that separates us from reaching our objective. When you give up too soon, you lose the opportunity to achieve great things.

They forget about their goals.

Today's business world operates at a frantic pace. We race to put out fires, we face new, unexpected challenges every day, and customers demand more from us. It is very easy to lose focus and forget about working on our goals. That is why writing down your goals every day is such a powerful strategy. It keeps them in our mind. It reminds us where our focus should be. It helps us remember to take action.

They try to accomplish everything on their own.

Surprisingly, many people think they have to work on their own to achieve their goals. This means they do not enlist the support or help of other people. We all have pride, but it is important to recognize that other people can help us achieve our goals. Friends, family, and business associates all possess knowledge that will move us forward. Networking and mastermind groups can provide valuable feedback. No one person has all the answers necessary to succeed in today's business climate.

When I started writing the first edition of this book, I spoke to several other authors to discuss the challenges they faced. I asked them for advice, and in every single situation, they were willing to share their expertise. I took the same approach when I left the security of a full-time job to start my own business. I talked to people who operate similar businesses and learned some of the common pitfalls as well as success strategies.

So far, we have discussed the reasons why people do not set goals and why they do not achieve the goals they do set. Let's look at some criteria on setting goals so you can achieve the best possible results.

Setting SMART Goals

When you decide to set goals use the SMART formula:
S – Specific
M – Motivational
A – Achievable, yet challenging
R – Relevant
T – Time-framed

Specific

Each of your goals must be as specific as possible. For example, setting a goal to increase your sales is a worthy target. However, phrasing it like this—"I want to increase my sales"—is not clear enough. Rephrasing this to "I want to sell $10,000 this month" or "I want to increase my sales by 10 percent compared to last month" is better. The more concise, and specific your goal, the more focused it will become.

Motivational

As noted previously, your goals must be motivating. If you typically sell $10,000 in an average month and your goal is to sell $10,500 this month, it will not be powerful enough for you to get excited about achieving it. However, if you set a target of selling $12,000 and becoming the top salesperson in the store, you will become more motivated to achieve that goal. I know salespeople who are solely motivated to be the top performer in their store each month. They do not set a specific dollar figure. Instead, they say, "I will have the highest sales in the store." They constantly monitor the sales figures of their co-workers and push themselves to stay ahead of them.

Achievable, Yet Challenging

Goals that are too easy to achieve will not keep you motivated. If they are too difficult to reach, you will become discouraged and lose your desire to work toward them. I believe that goals should have a 70 to 80 percent opportunity of success. Challenging targets will push you out of your comfort zone and cause you to learn and grow. Over the years I have discovered that we are capable of accomplishing much more than we think. I have set goals that seem completely unrealistic only to achieve them faster and sooner than I anticipated. An associate of mine encourages people to set wildly ambitious goals rather than cautiously optimistic targets. This approach causes people to think far beyond their current situation and dream big dreams.

Relevant

Goals must be deeply personal for you. They must be relevant to your specific situation and life. Avoid setting goals based on the opinion of other people. Determine what is important to you.

Time-Framed

Every goal must have a deadline—otherwise, it is only a dream. Deadlines create a sense of urgency and help move you forward. I often work on several projects at any given time. When I do not have a specific deadline, I tend to procrastinate and postpone working on them. However, setting targeted completion dates gives me the focus and sense of urgency needed to accomplish them.

Here are a few examples of SMART goals:

"To sell $15,000 by the end of July."

"To sell 250 units of SKU number 234 during November."

"To contact 20 new prospects this week."

"To acquire three new accounts worth at least $2,000 each by March 21."

Exercise

In your action planner, identify goals that are meaningful and important to you. Follow the SMART method outlined above. You may find this process challenging, particularly if you have not set goals in the past. I encourage you to complete this exercise before reading further.

Creating Action Plans

You have now recorded short-, mid- and long-term goals as well as one or two life goals. Let's discuss how to create action plans that will help you achieve these goals.

An action plan is a series of steps you need to take to achieve your goals. In most cases, each action step is actually a mini-goal that moves you closer to achieving your overall target. Here is an example:

Goal:
"To generate at least $30,000 in sales during the month of May." (For purposes of this example we will assume it is the beginning of May and that the sales associate generally sells approximately $25,000 each month.)

Action Steps:

1. Identify and contact 30 new prospective customers by the end of the week (May 7). Set an appointment with each person to demonstrate our new line of products.

2. Create a track sheet for the number of customers I talk to and my closing ratio by May 2.

3. Learn exactly how SKU #395 operates by May 3. This is the most popular product we currently stock.

4. Identify at least 10 qualifying questions to ask my customers by May 5. Recite these questions aloud a minimum of five times to become comfortable with them.

5. Seek feedback from Bill (top salesperson) by May 7 to find out how he handles the most difficult objections.

6. Watch Bill interact with his customers a minimum of once a day for the next two weeks (May 1-14).

7. Ask every customer for the sale every day.

8. Ask Bill to critique my approach at least twice a week until the end of the month.

Once you have created this action plan, get moving! Do not waste time wondering if your plan will work. Instead, tackle your list and begin moving forward. Don't worry if your action plan is not perfect. You can make adjustments as you move ahead. In fact, successful salespeople make changes to their plans on a regular basis. When you encounter obstacles or barriers—and you will—review your action plan and make the necessary changes that will enable you to overcome these challenges.

Many people are concerned about the time required for this entire process. Smart business people recognize the importance of planning and know that proper planning actually saves time down the road. Fewer mistakes are made; solutions for potential obstacles are developed. Detailed plans help everyone stay on track. I recommend investing one day per month for planning your goals and objectives. Use the first of the month to determine where you plan to go, what you want to achieve, and how you are going to get there. This small investment of time will quickly pay for itself.

Exercise

In your action planner, start creating action plans for each of your goals.

You have now identified several goals and created action plans for them. The last comment about achieving your goals is to be persistent.

Failure Is Not an Option

"Failure is not an option." When faced with adversity, repeat this mantra over and over again. The most successful people in every industry remain focused on how they will drive their business forward. When times are tough, they dig their heels in and look for creative ways to generate sales. They rarely think about giving up.

Vow to stay focused on accomplishing the goals you set for yourself regardless of what happens. I guarantee you will encounter resistance in the pursuit of your goals. Persistence, above anything else, will propel you forward and help you achieve your dreams. In fact, here is a poem I came across in Brian Tracy's book, *Maximum Achievement*, that expresses the importance of persistence:

> **Don't Quit**
> When things go wrong, as they sometimes will,
> When the roads you're trudging seem all uphill,
> When the funds are low and debts are high,
> And you want to smile but you have to sigh,
> When care is pressing you down quite a bit
> Rest if you must, but don't quit.
> For life is queer with its twists and turns,
> As every one of us sometimes learns,
> And many a failure runs about,
> When he might have won if he'd stuck it out.
> Success is just failure turned inside out,
> The silver tint of the clouds of doubt,
> And you never can tell how close you are,
> It may be near when it seems so far.
> So stick to the fight when you're hardest hit,
> It's when things seem worst that *you must not quit!*
> —Anonymous

Summary

1. Goals give you focus, clarity, and direction; powerful goals will keep you motivated.

2. Create goals that give you a sense of purpose. Follow the SMART formula—Specific, Motivational, Achievable, Relevant, Time-framed.

3. Record your goals on paper and write them out every day.

4. Create detailed action plans for each of your goals. Each action step should follow the SMART method.

5. Review your action plans regularly and make modifications and changes as necessary.

6. Be persistent. Do not give up.

Action Plan

In your action planner, answer the following questions:

1. What did you learn about setting goals that you did not know before reading this chapter?

2. What will you do differently starting today?

3. What challenges do you anticipate?

4. How will you address these challenges?

A–Z Qualifying

This appendix contains questions that are specific to different types of operations. I have listed over 400 different questions—mostly open-ended—for virtually every type of retail or business-to-consumer operation. These questions will help you determine your customers' needs and establish rapport with them.

Appliances

What are you looking for?
What features do you want?
What is important to you?
What colour appeals to you?
Tell me about the layout of your kitchen/laundry room.
What appliances do you currently have?
What would you like you new appliances to have/do that your current ones don't have/do?

Automobiles

What type of car most interests you? Why?
What features are most important to you?
What do you currently drive?
What do you like about it?
What would you like to change?
Approximately how much do you drive in an average week/year?
What type of driving do you do?

What are your thoughts about leasing versus buying?
Who else is involved in this decision?
What is important to them?
What have you looked at so far?
What prompted you to consider that vehicle?
How did you enjoy driving that particular vehicle?

Auto Repair/Collision

Tell me what happened.
Who will be paying for the repair?
What concerns do you have about this repair?
Who will be covering a rental vehicle?
How soon do you need the vehicle repaired?
What other shops have you brought your vehicle to?

Blinds, Shades, Shutters, and Awnings

Tell me about the room where the blinds are going.
Where will the awning be going?
Why are you looking for this now?
Who will be installing this/these?
What colour were you considering?
What style of blind/shade/shutter/awning were you looking for?
What prompted you to consider that particular style?
Where else have you looked?
What else have you seen?
What is important to you?

Carpet/Flooring

Where will the carpet be going?
How much traffic does the area get?
What are some of the most important considerations for you?
How long do you plan to own your home?
What is currently in place?
What type of carpet pile would you like?
How much moisture is the area typically exposed to?
Who will be doing the installation?
Who do you want to remove the existing carpet/flooring?
How do you plan to dispose of the existing carpet/flooring?
What colour of tile/carpet/flooring do you want?

Cell Phones

Tell me what you currently have.
Why are you looking for a new phone?
What features do you want?
How do you use your phone?
What do you like about your current phone?
What would you like to see changed?
How much traveling do you do?
Where do you travel to?
When do you make most of your calls?

Computers

Tell me about your current computer.
What does your current set-up consist of?
What were you looking for in a new computer?
How do you use you computer in an average week?
What would you like your computer to do that it isn't doing now?
Who else uses the computer?
What is important to them?
How long have you had your existing computer?
What prompted you to look for a new computer?
What changes have you made in the way you use your computer?

Cycle Shops

What do you currently have?
How long have you owned it?
How much do you bike in an average week?
What type of terrain do you generally bike on?
What do you normally wear when cycling?
How long are your rides?
What do you do in the off-season?
How did you get involved in this sport?

Dance Studios

What style of dance most appeals to you? Why?
What experience do you have?
Have you been a member of another studio in the past?
What prompted you to leave?

What other studios have you talked to?
What are your expectations?
Is an end-of-the-year recital important to you?

Electronics

What do you currently have?
How will you be using the . . . ?
What do you want the product to do for you?
What experience do you have with this type of product?
How do you see yourself using this in the future?
What do you know about the product/technology?
Tell me about your current set-up.
What kind of music do you prefer?
What are some of your favourite movies?
What else have you seen?

Financial Planners

What are your long-term/short-term financial goals?
What do you currently contribute to retirement?
What is your level of risk?
What concerns do you have about investing your money?
What is important to you?
How involved do you want to be with your investing?
What lifestyle goals do you have for when you are 45? 55? 65?
How much traveling would you like to do?
How do you see yourself spending your time when you retire?
What other types of investments do you have?
Who else do you invest with?
What has been your experience with financial planners?
What do you expect from your financial planner?

Fitness Centres

What prompted you to consider joining a fitness club?
What are your fitness goals?
How many times a week do you plan to visit the club?
How will you fit this into your schedule?
What do you expect from us?

What previous experience do you have with fitness centres?
What would you like to achieve?
Have you considered working with a personal trainer? Nutritionist?

Golf Products

Tell me about your current set of clubs.
How often do you play?
What type of courses do you usually play?
How long have you been playing?
What prompted you to look for a new set of clubs?
What kind of balls do you usually use?
What type of bag do you currently have?
What kind of shoes do you wear?
What aspect of your game would you most like to improve?

Hair Salons/Stylists

What are you looking for in a new style?
What is important to you? Why?
How much time do you want to spend styling your hair each day?
What colour appeals to you?
What products do you currently use?
How often do you change products?
What do you look for in a product?

Health/Nutrition Products

What supplements do you currently use?
What results have you experienced?
What are your goals with respect to your health?
What prompted you to shop for these supplements?
Where else do you shop for these types of products?
How long have you been using these kinds of products?
What vitamins do you usually take?
Do you belong to a gym?
Tell me about your exercise routine.
What type of exercise program are you involved with?
What has your experience been in the past?
What concerns do you have?

Home Furnishings

Tell me a bit about your living room/kitchen/bedroom/patio/backyard?
What brings you into our store today?
What prompted you to shop for this particular item?
Tell me about your favourite decorations at home.
Tell me about the colour scheme in your home.
What style of furniture do you have?
How often do you buy items like this?

Home Renovations

What look do you want?
What is important to you with this renovation?
What colour of . . . do you prefer?
What prompted you to do this renovation?
What do you want to achieve with it?
Who else have you talked to?
What time frame were you looking at?
What budget have you established?
What type of fixtures/flooring/cabinets/lighting/counters appeal to you?
How much of this will you be doing yourself?
Have you ever done a renovation before?

Interior Design

What changes would you like to make?
What colours do you prefer?
What colours do you not like?
What patterns do you prefer?
Tell me what outcome you would like to see/have.
Have you worked with an interior designer in the past?
What was your experience?
What concerns do you have?
Who else have you talked to?
What budget have you established for this?
What kind of time frame are we working with?

Jewelry

What brings you into our store today?
What price range did you have in mind?

Tell me what type of jewelry you/she/he currently has.
What is the occasion?
When was the last time you bought something like this?
What do you want him/her to say when they receive this?
What is important to you with this purchase?
What do you think is important to him/her?
What concerns do you have about this purchase?

Kitchens

What style of cabinet most appeals to you?
What prompted you to make these changes?
What have you talked about so far?
What are some of the features you would like a new kitchen to have?
Why are those important to you?
When were you hoping to have this completed?
How much of the work do you expect to do?
What have you seen that you particularly liked?

Lawn care/Landscaping

What would you like your lawn to look like?
How much interest do you have in gardening?
Who will be responsible for the upkeep?
What have you seen that you like/dislike?
How often do you want to plant new flowers?
How often do you cut your lawn/prune your plants or trees?
Who is your current pest control company?
What has your experience been so far?
How active are in you in the maintenance of your lawn?

Lighting

Tell me what you currently have.
What would you like to change? Why?
Who will do the installation?
What other lighting do you have?
What made you decide to make this change?

Luggage

How much traveling do you typically do?

What specific features are you looking for?
What products have you owned in the past?
What was your experience with those products?
Who else travels with you?
What colour appeals to you?
What is most important to you? Why?
How much walking do you do with your luggage?

Men's Fashion

Suits:
When do you normally wear a suit?
How often do you wear a suit?
What type of traveling do you typically do?
What image do you want to present?
What styles appeal to you?
What particular colour did you have in mind?

Shirts:
What will you match the shirt with?
What patterns do you prefer?
What style of shirt most interests you?
What style of cuffs do you like?
What blend of fabric do you like?
What kind of collar do you want?
What colours most interest you?

Ties:
How often do you wear a tie?
What do you normally wear it with?
What colour shirt will you be matching this tie with?
How conservative or adventurous are you?
Tell me about the ties you currently have in your collection.

Pants/Trousers:
What colour do you prefer?
What do you normally wear with your dress pants?
How often do you wear them?
To what type of occasion do you wear dress pants?
Tell me what you currently have.
What is important to you? Why?

Music Equipment

What type of instrument do you currently own?
How long have you been playing?
How did you get started?
How often do you play?
Tell me where you usually play.
What is your favourite type of music?
Why are you looking for a new...?
How long have you had your existing instrument?
What do you like least/most about it?
What kind of microphone do you use?
What other equipment do you have?
How long have you owned it?
What brand of cables/cords do you use to hook up your equipment?

Nutritionists

What prompted you to use a nutritionist?
Have you worked with a nutritionist before?
What are your expectations?
How quickly do you expect to see results?
What do you want to achieve?

Office Supplies

How do you plan to use this in a typical week?
What line of work are you in?
How long have you been in business?
What other products do you use?
What else can you picture yourself using?
How large is your office?
How many people do you have working for you?

Opticians

What style of eyewear most appeals to you?
When do you typically wear glasses?
What do you wear when it is sunny outside?
How many pairs of glasses have you owned?
What prompted you to consider contact lenses?

Paint, Wallpaper, and Wall Coverings

What do you currently have on your walls?
How long has this been in place?
What would you like to change?
What treatment(s) most interest you?
Who will be involved in the decorating?
Tell me about your likes and dislikes.
What colours do you prefer?
What are some of your favourite patterns?
When were you planning to do this?
What other items do you need?
What concerns you most about this change?

Party Supplies

What do you have planned for this event?
How many people will be invited/attending?
What do you think will be most important to . . . ?
What other items have you considered using?

Patio Furniture

What do you currently have?
How much time do you spend in your backyard?
How many people typically visit at any given time?
What meals do you eat outside?
Tell me about the area where the furniture will be going.
How do you normally store your furniture during the winter?

Pets

What pets do you currently have?
What pets have you owned in the past?
What prompted you to consider buying a . . . ?
What do you know about the care of . . . ?
Who else will be involved in the care and maintenance of the . . . ?
What equipment do you own?

Quilts

What type of quilt would you like?
Have you owned a quilt before?

How will you be using it?
Where will the quilt be going?
What are your favourite/least favourite colours?

Real Estate

What are you looking for in a new home?
What area of the city would you most like to live in?
What is important to you?
How large is your family?
Where do you work? Do you plan to commute?
What features do you want in a home?
Why are those important to you?
How do you currently get around the city?

Running Wear

How much do you run in an average week?
Where do you usually run?
Tell me about your runs in an average week.
How do you stay hydrated during your long runs?
Who do you run with?
What races have you run in the past?
What brand of shoes have you owned in the past?
What has been your experience with them?
What clothing do you typically wear?
At what time of the day do you usually run?
Have you ever been injured? What happened?
What do you use to time or measure your runs?
What type of socks do you normally wear when running?

Security Alarms

Why do you want a security system?
What is important to you?
Who will be operating the system?
Tell me about your daily routine.
What concerns do you have about this?

Swimming Pools

What prompted you to buy a swimming pool?

What style of pool were you considering?
Who will be doing most of the installation?
How large is your yard?
Tell me about your yard.
How many children do you have?
What are their ages?
Will you be remodeling the rest of the yard as well?
Who will be doing those changes?
What is your experience with pools?
What type of deck were you thinking about?
What kind of fence do you have? How high is it?
Tell me about the accessibility of your backyard.

Travel Agents

What would you like to do on your vacation?
What type of vacation appeals to you? Leisure? Activity-based?
What destination did you have in mind? Why?
How long a trip were you planning?
Who else will be going with you?
Where were you planning to go?
What is your favourite mode of transportation?
What style of hotel do you prefer?
What type of restaurants do you like?
Have you been on a trip like this before?
What was your experience?

Upholstery

What type of fabric would you like?
What colours were you thinking about?
What time frame are we working with?
How soon did you need the furniture returned?
Have you ever had furniture reupholstered?
What concerns do you have?
Do you need us to pick up and drop off the furniture?

Vacuums

What do you currently have?
How long have you owned that particular model?

How satisfied have you been?
What is important to you?
Who usually does the vacuuming?
How large is your household?
What type of flooring do you have?
How many stairs are in your house?

Wines

What type of wines do you prefer?
What kinds of meals do you enjoy wine with?
How often do you drink wine?
On what kinds of occasions do you usually drink wine?
What are your favourite foods?
With what foods do you typically drink wine?
Do you have a wine cellar?
What type of cellar do you have?
How many bottles do you have in your cellar?
What price range are the wines in your cellar?
How many bottles do you plan to expand your cellar to?

Women's Fashion

Dresses:
What do you look for in a dress?
What types of occasions do you wear a dress on?
What do you usually wear with it?
Tell me about the dresses you have in your closet.
What accessories do you normally add?
How often do you wear a dress?

Blouses:
What were you looking for in a blouse?
What will you wear it with?
What kind of fabric do you prefer?
Tell me what kind of blouses you currently have.
How often do you plan to wear this?
How much traveling do you do?
What is important to you with this purchase?

Accessories:
What specifically are you looking for?
What will you wear this with?
What other types of accessories do you have?
What colour of clothing do you typically wear/buy?

Shoes:
When will you be wearing these?
What will you wear these shoes with?
How long will you wear them on a typical day?
What style of heel do you prefer?
How much of a heel do you like?
Tell me about the shoes you have in your closet.

100 Ways to Increase Your Sales

1. The First Rule of Life: develop and maintain a positive attitude. Your success in sales and life depends on it.

2. Know your products; become an expert on them.

3. Practise your presentation; role-play and videotape yourself if possible.

4. Involve your customers. Engage them in the entire process. Don't force them to be passive bystanders.

5. Learn your customer's name and use it.

6. Establish your credibility early by asking effective questions and actively listening to your customer's answers and concerns.

7. Use eye contact to establish rapport.

8. Learn as much about your competition as you can.

9. Anticipate potential problems and prepare possible responses.

10. Check your inventory in advance. Know what you have available to sell.

11. Obtain information about your customers by asking them questions.

12. Teach yourself to relax; breathe deeply, meditate, use positive self-talk with yourself.

13. Learn the steps to selling and use them every day.

14. Manage your time properly. Invest time promoting your business.

15. Rest so you are physically and psychologically alert.

16. Use your own style—don't imitate someone else.

17. Use your own words—don't recite from memory.

18. Put yourself in the customer's shoes. Remember WII-FM—What's In It For Me?

19. Assume the customer is on your side.

20. Tell the customers that you want to take time to identify their needs.

21. Identify your fears. Categorize them as controllable or uncontrollable and confront them.

22. Develop a great smile and use it.

23. Introduce yourself to your customer with a social or a merchandise-focused opening.

24. Give special emphasis to the first few minutes you spend with each customer. You won't get a second chance to make a first impression.

25. Visualize yourself as a *successful* retail salesperson.

26. Manage your image and personal appearance.

27. Decide that you will make more presentations than anyone else every day.

28. Know where everything is that you need to do your job. Don't waste your time or your customer's time looking for a piece of information or set of instructions.

29. Relax and enjoy yourself. Have fun with your customers.

30. No one sells to *every* customer. Learn how to hand over a customer you are unable to close a sale with to another salesperson.

31. Believe in yourself first. If you don't think you can make the sale, who will?

32. Set and achieve goals. A goal is simply a dream with a deadline and a plan of action.

33. Learn the fundamental concepts of selling and use them. Read, attend seminars, listen to tapes, and adapt the recommended techniques to your style.

34. Learn one new technique a week. Put it into practice as soon as you learn it.

35. Use your car as a learning centre. A how-to sales tape or CD does more for your success than the radio.

36. Visualize the sale taking place before it happens.

37. Shake hands with customers firmly. No one wants to shake hands with a dead fish.

38. Be conversational in your presentation. Speak as though you are talking with a friend.

39. Develop great telephone skills.

40. Don't prejudge people; they are often customers in disguise.

41. Understand your customers and meet their needs. Question and listen actively to uncover their true needs.

42. Sell to assist your customers; don't sell for money.

43. Do a regular self-analysis. Determine what you want to achieve, both long term and short term, in your career.

44. Believe in the company and your product or service. If you don't, your customer won't either. If you believe in what you're selling, that confidence will show.

45. Be prepared with questions, answers, statements, openers.

46. Try new approaches. Don't get trapped into doing everything the same way all the time.

47. Listen carefully to how your customer answers your questions.

48. Adapt your presentation to meet your customer's needs.

49. Learn how to present yourself effectively. Take a course in public speaking or join a local chapter of Toastmasters International.

50. Show your customers that you differ from your competitors; don't just tell them.

51. Subscribe to trade magazines to learn more about your specific industry.

52. Pay attention to your customers. Make them feel important.

53. Start work half an hour earlier and stay half an hour later.

54. Spend less time socializing and more time working when you're on the job.

55. Invest more time learning about your customer.

56. Learn to ask more open-ended questions.

57. Demonstrate to your customer the value of buying from you and your store.

58. Learn to empathize.

59. Clarify your customer's objections.

60. Ask every customer for the sale.

61. Don't allow the first objection to bring the sales process to a halt.

62. Keep your name in your customer's mind. Stay in touch with that customer after the sale.

63. Ask every customer for a referral.

64. Follow up every sale with a thank-you call.

65. Send every customer a thank-you card.

66. Learn to accessorize every sale.

67. Be the expert that your customers can trust.

68. Learn to become comfortable with silence.

69. Be quiet after you ask for the sale.

70. Be quiet after you ask your customer a question.

71. Spend less time waiting for customers to come into your store and invest more time seeking them out.

72. Invest more time qualifying customers instead of presenting to them.

73. View the sales interaction as a process, not an event.

74. Don't rush.

75. Be proactive in everything you do. Don't wait for a customer to ask for something.

76. Listen more than you talk.

77. Maintain your motivation by listening to or reading inspirational material each day.

78. Give people a reason to buy from you. Be able to answer, "Why should I buy from you?"

79. Know what products your competitors carry and how they differ from yours.

80. Give the customer who comes into the store at 8:30 p.m. the same attention you gave your first customer that day.

81. Make no assumptions.

82. Think before you speak.

83. Do more than your share of work in the store.

84. Don't take objections personally. Find out the real objection.

85. Vary your greeting. Don't use the standard, "Hi, how are you?"

86. Focus on uncovering your customer's emotional needs.

87. Vary your tone of voice. Avoid slipping into a monotone.

88. Use different closing techniques.

89. Seek a customer's permission before you offer him a solution to an objection.

90. Make sure your solutions are appropriate to each customer. Avoid giving canned answers.

91. Don't complain about things that are beyond your control.

92. Don't get discouraged—every "no" you hear gets you one step closer to "yes."

93. Watch the top-performing people in your store. Notice what they do differently and then adapt their behaviours to fit your style.

94. Stay in touch with your customers.

95. Evaluate your strengths and areas that need improvement on a daily basis.

96. Be aware of your customer's fears and hesitations.

97. Treat each customer differently.

98. Treat every customer with dignity and respect.

99. Give people a reason to buy from you, today, at your price.

100. STOP, ASK, and LISTEN.

a p p e n d i x 3

A Blueprint for Success

After attending my training workshops, participants used to return to their stores and eagerly try to apply the concepts laid out in this program. Often, their efforts lacked focus and direction. They would try to apply all the concepts at once without mastering *any* of them. I soon realized that unless they had a clear plan to follow, they would not be able to make the most of their efforts or reap the appropriate rewards.

Here is a step-by-step plan to help you apply the concepts covered in this book. The idea behind the blueprint is simple. I am going to ask you to try to master one skill before you move to applying another one. You will build on the skills you develop. For one week you will concentrate on applying one, and only one, of these concepts. Each week you will record your results before moving on to the next concept. If you carefully execute what you have read, if you apply what you have learned, if you follow this blueprint, you will harvest tremendous rewards.

Over time you will notice that people will respond to you differently. Customers will divulge more information to you. They will seem more at ease with you. You will develop more trust and rapport with them. You will overcome objections more effectively. You will feel more confident in asking for the sale. You will be able to outshine your co-workers. You will close more sales! You will make more money!

The key to making this blueprint work is to tackle the challenging concepts with as much enthusiasm as you do the more enjoyable tasks. Recognize that becoming a retail superstar is not very difficult as long as you are willing to work at it. Discipline yourself to follow through on this process completely. Use your time management system or to-do list to record specific steps you intend to complete each day. Focus on becoming the best salesperson you possibly can. Demonstrate to all the customers you deal with why they should buy from you, today, at your price.

Finally, I suggest that you keep track of your results each week. You should notice a steady increase. Obviously, not every week will indicate growth since many external variables can influence sales from day to day. However, you should notice an improvement overall as you move through the process.

Right now I will tell you that you will find it difficult to follow this process. You will be distracted, or too busy, or you might forget. Whatever the reason, if you miss a week, simply pick up where you left off before the interruption or distraction, and carry on with the program. Similarly, when you return from a vacation, pick up where you left off and go on. The investment will take effort, energy, and discipline. It will require dedication and commitment. It will present you with more challenges and obstacles than you might have noticed in your work before. I also guarantee that the program will work for you.

Most self-help or sales books will provide you with lots of great information, but they don't help you learn how to apply it. *Stop, Ask and Listen* maps out a success route for you. My goal is to help you become as successful as possible, to reach your full potential, to capitalize on your opportunities and maximize your sales results. In fact, as part of this commitment, please feel free to email with your questions or concerns. I am more than willing to provide additional support and feedback to help you in your quest to become a sales superstar. Email your question to Kelley@RobertsonTrainingGroup.com and I will respond within a day or two. You can also visit my website and sign up for the

59-Second Tip, a weekly e-zine that provides one piece of practical sales advice every week. There is no cost and you can unsubscribe at any time. Log on to www.StopAskListen.com to sign up.

Are you ready? Now you can begin to implement what you have learned! Good luck!

Blueprint for Success

Week	Concept or Skill	How to Implement It
1	Vary your greeting.	Vary your greeting with every customer who enters your store. Avoid the standard, "Hi, how are you today?" Use different greetings. Employ humour to overcome the "Just Looking" response.
2	Build rapport.	Get your customers to relax and feel comfortable with you by asking questions that focus on them. Encourage them to talk about their interests.
3	Ask open-ended questions.	Review the list of open-ended questions near the end of Chapter Four and in Appendix One. Determine which questions are appropriate to your business and concentrate on using them.
4	Discuss benefits.	Demonstrate the benefit of the products you are selling. When you begin to show a product to a customer, concentrate on discussing the benefits rather than the features. Say, "And this one has . . . which means that . . . " Remember, people buy benefits, not features.
5	Paint mental pictures.	Get people excited by painting mental pictures. Review the list of descriptive words you developed in Chapter Five. Begin using a variety of different words when you discuss your products or services with customers.

Week	Concept or Skill	How to Implement It
6	Create unique presentation tools.	Make time to create some unique tools. Use these to enhance your presentations and set yourself apart from your competition.
7	Empathize and clarify.	Every time you hear a customer express an objection, first empathize, then clarify. "I can appreciate that; most people like to think about their purchase before committing themselves. What is it exactly that you'd like to think about?" Repeat the process as often as it takes to uncover the customer's real objection. Memorize your scripts for the most common objections. Repeat them until you feel comfortable saying them. Then use one when you hear that objection. Repeat the process for each objection.
8	Seek permission.	Show your customers respect by asking permission to offer a solution. "Would it be okay if I took a moment to explain some of the benefits of buying from us?" When they respond positively, keep your solution as brief as possible. Ideally, you should talk for less than 20 seconds.
9	Ask for the sale.	Ask every customer for the sale. Remain silent until they respond, regardless of how long it takes.
10	Accessorize.	Suggest accessories for everything you sell. Don't stop selling accessories until the customer asks you to stop.
11	Ask for a referral.	Ask every customer for a referral. "If you've been happy with the service I've provided and know someone who could benefit, have them give me a call." Then hand them a business card. Maintain a positive, confident body positioning to add credibility to your request.

Week	Concept or Skill	How to Implement It
12	Follow up.	Follow up with your customers. Contact them by phone a few days after their initial purchase and thank them for doing business with you. Don't try to sell them anything more. Just demonstrate that you are differentfrom your competition and give people a reason to return to your store and purchase from you.

The following pages explain how to set up your own plan and record the weekly implementation process. You can also print worksheets from www.StopAskListen.com. Here you will note your results every week and answer some questions. The questions will encourage you to reflect on the previous week, to think about what you did and what results you achieved. They will help you analyze and document your progress.

Discipline yourself to complete each week's assignment and complete the weekly reviews. I guarantee you'll notice results!

Week 1—Vary Your Greeting

Vary your greeting with every customer who enters your store. Avoid the standard, "Hi, how are you today?" Use different greetings. Seek methods to avoid and/or overcome the "Just Looking" response. Consider Good afternoon, welcome to ..." or "It looks like you're in a hurry. What can I do to help?"

Weekly Review (complete at the end of the week)

Sales: $ _____

What new greetings did you use?
How did these greetings change the way your customers responded to you?
What impact did they make on your overall results?

What did you find easy or difficult about this week's exercise?
What will you do differently next week?

Continue varying your greetings with all your customers. Become comfortable using a variety of merchandise-focused and social greetings.

Week 2—Build Rapport

Get your customers to relax with you by asking questions that focus on them. Encourage them to talk about their interests. Pay attention to what is important to your customers. Listen to what they tell you.

Weekly Review (complete at the end of the week)

Sales: $ _____

How did you work at building rapport with your customers?
How did your customers respond?
How did this approach influence your overall performance?
What challenges did you encounter?
What will you do differently next week?

Continue establishing rapport with your customers. Search for areas of common interest. Recognize that you will not be able to achieve this with every customer. Don't allow these people to prevent you from building rapport with other customers.

Week 3—Ask Open-Ended Questions

Review the list of open-ended questions in Chapter Four. Determine which questions are appropriate to your business and concentrate on using them. Consider questions such as

"What features are you looking for in a . . . ?"
"Why are you buying a . . . ?"
"When were you planning to make this purchase?"

Then be quiet and listen to the customer's response. Spend 80 percent of your time listening and only 20 percent talking.

Weekly Review (complete at the end of the week)

Sales: $ _____

What percentage of the questions you asked were open-ended?
What difficulties did you experience?
How did you deal with these challenges?
What impact did asking open-ended questions have on your overall results?

Continue to concentrate on asking open-ended questions. This process can be very challenging, because we habitually ask closed-ended questions in everyday conversations. Keep reviewing your list of open-ended questions; become comfortable using these questions; listen to yourself; learn how to ask an open-ended question in any situation.

Week 4—Discuss Benefits
Demonstrate the benefit of the products you're selling. When you begin to show a product to a customer, focus on discussing its benefits instead of its features. Say, "And this one has ... which means that . . . " Remember that people buy benefits, not features.

Weekly Review (complete at the end of the week)

Sales: $ _____

How easy or difficult was it to discuss the benefits instead of the features?
What influence did this approach have on your overall performance?
What challenges did you encounter?
What did you do to overcome these challenges?
Where do you feel you need to improve?
What do you plan to do differently?

Continue to discuss the benefits specific features offer. Show and tell your customers how your product or service will make their life easier, more satisfying, more productive, or more enjoyable. Give them a compelling reason to buy from you.

Week 5—Paint Mental Pictures
Get people excited by painting mental pictures. Review the list of descriptive words you developed in Chapter Five. Begin using a variety of different words when you discuss your products or services with customers.

Weekly Review (complete at the end of the week)

Sales: $ _____

What descriptive words did you use this past week?
What types of responses did you receive from your customers?
What impact did this have on your overall results?
What challenges did you face and how did you deal with them?
What will you do differently next week?

Continue painting mental pictures for your customers. Expand your vocabulary by brainstorming with your co-workers. Create phrases that conjure up vivid images and that stir the imagination.

Week 6—Create Unique Presentation Tools
Make the time to create some unique tools for yourself. Use these tools to enhance your presentations and set yourself apart from your competition.

Weekly Review (complete at the end of the week)

Sales: $ _____

What tools did you develop?
How did you use them?
What response or reaction did you get from your customers?
How did they influence your overall results?
How will you use these tools in the upcoming weeks?

Continue using these tools to enhance your presentations and develop additional tools. Look for new and creative ways to make yourself stand out from your competition. Give people a reason to buy from you, today, at your price!

Week 7—Empathize and Clarify
Every time you hear a customer express an objection, first empathize with him or her, then clarify. "I can appreciate that; most people like to think about their purchase before committing themselves. What is it exactly that you'd like to think about?" Repeat the process as often as it takes to uncover the real objection. Memorize your scripts for the most common

objections. Repeat them until you feel comfortable saying them. Then use them when you hear that objection. Repeat the process for each objection.

Weekly Review (complete at the end of the week)

Sales: $ —————————————

What objection responses did you use most often?
Did you feel comfortable empathizing and clarifying?
Did you memorize your response until you could recite it perfectly?
What do you need to do to improve?
What will you do differently next week?

Continue empathizing and clarifying when you hear objections. This is a very difficult process for most people when they begin. If you practise it repeatedly, you will become more comfortable with it. The empathy statement will directly reflect the feelings the customer is experiencing and the clarifying question will uncover the real objection. Don't give up! You've come this far; keep at it!

Week 8—Seek Permission
Show your customers respect by asking permission to offer a solution. "Would it be okay if I took a moment to explain some of the benefits of buying from us?" When they respond positively, keep your solution as brief as possible. Aim to talk for less than 20 seconds.

Weekly Review (complete at the end of the week)

Sales: $ —————————————

How easy or difficult was this concept to implement?
What type of response did you receive from customers when you asked permission to provide a solution?
How did this change the way you presented a solution?
How did this approach affect your overall results?
Where could you improve?

Continue asking customers for their permission to overcome their objections. This demonstrates your respect for their opinion.

Maintain a non-threatening tone of voice as well as great eye contact. Be optimistic about the outcome of your requesting this permission.

Week 9—Ask for the Sale

Ask every customer for the sale. Remain silent until he or she responds no matter how long a customer takes to answer you.

Weekly Review (complete at the end of the week)

Sales: $ _____

What percentage of customers did you ask for the sale?
Was this easy to do? Explain.
Were you able to remain silent until the customer responded?
What was the longest you had to wait in silence?
How did this approach affect your overall results?
What will you do differently next week?

Continue asking every customer for the sale. You ask; you receive. You don't ask; you don't receive. After you ask a customer for the sale, remain silent until he or she responds. Keep practising this until you become comfortable with long periods of silence.

Week 10—Accessorize

Suggest accessories for everything you sell. Continue selling accessories until the customer tells you to stop.

Weekly Review (Complete at the end of the week)

Sales: $_____

How were your accessory sales this week?
What response did you receive from customers when you asked them
to purchase additional items?
What went well?
What could be improved?
What will you do differently next week?

Continue suggesting accessories. Qualify your customers thoroughly to determine their specific needs, and use accessories to help meet those needs. You need not be pushy; you do need to be assertive. Recognize and remember that people want to fully enjoy and use the products and services they buy. Accessories enhance and make this possible!

Week 11—Ask for a Referral

Ask all customers for referrals. "If you've been happy with the service I've provided and know someone who could benefit, have them give me a call." Then hand the customer a business card. Maintain positive, confident body positioning to add credibility to your request.

Weekly Review (complete at the end of the week)

Sales: $ ———————————

How difficult was it for you to ask for a referral?
What type of response did you get from your customers?
How did this influence your overall results?
Where could you improve?
What do you plan to do about it?

Continue to ask every customer for a referral. Remember that people experience a flood of emotions when they make a purchase, and many times they want to share this experience with others. Every referral you generate can translate into another sale.

Week 12—Follow up

Follow up with your customers. Contact them by phone a few days after their initial purchase and thank them for doing business with you. Don't try to sell them anything more. Just demonstrate that you are different from your competition; give people a reason to return to your store and buy more from you.

Weekly Review (complete at the end of the week)

Sales: $ ———————————

How many customers did you contact this week after you sold them a product/service?
What type of response did they have?
What obstacles did you face and how did you deal with them?

What will you do differently in the future?

Follow-up with your customer will become more challenging as you get busier. Use some form of time management system to schedule specific activities and to remind you of them.

A Final Comment

You have just worked your way through a three-month process. If you disciplined yourself to follow the implementation schedule consistently, then you deserve a pat on the back for your effort, commitment, dedication, and hard work.

By now you have seen a change in your results. Today your interactions with customers are probably more relaxed, and your clients feel more comfortable with you. I will also bet that your ability to determine needs is much more developed and refined. You are keeping your customers' attention better during your presentations. You are finding customers' objections easier to overcome. Your sales have surely increased. Finally, you must be feeling much more confident about yourself as a successful salesperson than you did just 90 days ago.

Now I suggest that you return to the beginning of the Stop, Ask, and Listen implementation plan and complete the entire process again. In my experience, we can always use a refresher, regardless of how long we have been doing something. You'll find that you will have forgotten certain concepts. You'll notice that you'll come up with new ideas on how to implement other concepts. You'll also discover that you've mastered others. Keep mastering your skills and remember to Stop, Ask, and Listen!

Resources

No sales book would be complete without additional resource materials. Here are a few of my favourite books:

Sales

Advanced Selling Strategies, Brian Tracy, Simon & Schuster, 1995

GenderSell — How to Sell to the Opposite Sex, Judith Tingley, Lee E. Robert, Simon & Schuster, 1999

High Probability Selling, Jacques Werth, ABBA Publishing Company, 2000

Selling to VITO, Anthony Parinello, Adams Media, 1999

Seven Figure Selling, Danielle Kennedy, Berkely Business Books, 1996

Stop Telling, Start Selling, Linda Richardson, McGraw Hill, 1998

The 80% Minority, Joanne Thomas Yaccato, Viking Canada, 2003

Think and Sell Like a CEO, Anthony Parinello, Entrepreneur Press, 2002

What Women Want, Mary Lou Quinlan, John Wiley, 2003

Customer Service

Customers for Life, Carl Sewell, Doubleday, 1990

Dealing with the Customer From Hell, Shaun Belding, Stoddart, 2000

Delivering Knock Your Socks Off Service, Ron Zemke and Kirstin Anderson, AMACOM, 1991

How to Win Customers and Keep Them for Life, Michael LeBoeuf, Berkley Books, 1987

Just Say Yes! Philip R. Nulman, Career Press, 2000

Positively Outrageous Service, T. Scott Gross, Warner Books, 1991

The Myth of Excellence, Fred Crawford, Crown Publishing, 2001

Negotiating

Getting to Yes, Roger Fisher and William Ury, Penguin Books, 1983

Guerrilla Negotiating, Jay Conrad Levinson, John Wiley, 1999

Sales Negotiation Skills That Sell, Robert Kellar, AMACOM, 1997

Secrets of Power Negotiating for Salespeople, Roger Dawson, Career Press, 1999

The Total Negotiator, Stephen Pollan and Mark Levine, Avon Books, 1994

Marketing

Confessions of Shameless Self-Promoters, Debbie Allen, Success Showcase Publishing, 2002

Secrets of Power Marketing, George Torok and Peter Urs Bender, Stoddart Publishing, 2000

Communication

Communicate with Confidence, Dianna Booher, McGraw Hill, 1994

Men Are from Mars, Women Are from Venus, John Gray, Harper Collins, 1994

Secrets of Face-to-Face Communication, Dr. Robert Tracz and Peter Urs Bender, Stoddart Publishing, 2001

The Hidden Profit Center, Helen Wilkie, MHW Communications, 2003

Personal Growth & Leadership

A Tale of Two Employees, Chris Bart, Corporate Missions Inc. Press, 2002

Growing the Distance, Jim Clemmer, TCG Press, 1999

Maximum Achievement, Brian Tracy, Simon & Schuster, 1993

The Aladdin Factor, Jack Canfield and Mark Victor Hansen, Berkley Books, 1995

The Leader's Digest, Jim Clemmer, TCG Press, 2003

The 7 Habits of Highly Effective People, Stephen Covey, Simon & Schuster, 1989

Who Moved My Cheese? Spencer Johnson, G.P. Putman, 1995

Why Employees Don't Do What They're Supposed to Do and What to do About it, Ferdinand Fournies, McGraw Hill, 1999

Index

Want More?

Kelley Robertson is available for keynote presentations, conferences and workshops. If you manage a sales team, retail organization, or small business, you will benefit from his programs. He speaks on sales, negotiating, sales management, employee motivation, creating world class teams, and customer service. For information, call 905-633-7750, or e-mail your request to info@RobertsonTrainingGroup.com.

This book is suitable as a gift or incentive to your team members or to complement an in-house training program. Discounts are available for purchases of multiple copies. Call 905-633-7750 or e-mail sales@RobertsonTrainingGroup.com. You can also contact the publisher at 416-236-4433 for details.

Kelley also publishes the *59 Second Tip*, a free weekly e-zine that provides practical sales advice. To sign up for this newsletter visit www.RobertsonTrainingGroup.com.

Money-Back Guarantee

I am so convinced the principles presented in *Stop, Ask, and Listen* will help you, I am offering a money-back guarantee.

If, after implementing the concepts in the book, you fail to notice a positive increase in your sales or the manner in which your customers respond to you, you may return the book for full refund—no questions asked.

Simply return the book along with your proof of purchase to:

> Kelley Robertson
> Appleby Postal Outlet, Box 80044
> 4524 New Street
> Burlington, ON L7L 6B1

Because this is a personal guarantee, your local bookstore will not honour this commitment. Therefore, please *do not* return the book to the store.

Please allow four to six weeks for reimbursement.

About the Author

Kelley Robertson, President of The Robertson Training Group, has been helping people improve their skills for almost fifteen years. He began by training employees, managers and owner/operators in the hospitality industry, and then became Manager of Retail Training for Sony of Canada. Since 1995, he has conducted hundreds of training workshops and helped thousands of professionals improve their sales results.

His growing client list includes the Canadian Franchise Association, Crabtree & Evelyn, Delta Hotels, Hillebrand Estates Winery, Home Hardware, Rogers AT&T Wireless, Rogers Video, Sony of Canada, and Staples/Business Depot.

Kelley Robertson's articles are frequently published in a variety of online and print magazines and newsletters, such as, *Selling Power*, *Training*, *Sales & Marketing*, *Sales Promotion*, *Canadian Business Franchise*, *Small Business Canada*, *Creative Training Techniques*, and *Executive Sales Briefing*. His column appears regularly in *Canadian Vending* magazine, and his weekly newsletter, *The 59-Second Tip*, provides insight on a wide variety of business skills.

Kelley Robertson can be reached at:
kelley@robertsontraininggroup.com